HIDDEN ULSTER

DISCARD

HIDDEN ULSTER

Protestants & the Irish Language

PÁDRAIG Ó SNODAIGH

LAGAN PRESS
BELFAST
1995

Published by
Lagan Press
PO Box 110 BT12 4AB, Belfast
in conjunction with
Iontaobhas Ultach/The Ultach Trust
Fountain House, Donegall Place, Belfast

The publishers wish to acknowledge the financial assistance
of the Cultural Traditions Group in the production of this book.

ISBN: 1 873687 35 4
Author: Ó Snodaigh, Pádraig
Title: Hidden Ulster
Subtitle: Protestants and the Irish Language
1995

Front cover: *The Belfast Harp Festival, 1792*
(a late 19th-century impression, reversed)
Cover design: December Publications
Set in New Baskerville
Printed by Noel Murphy Printing, Belfast

*i gcuimhne mo Bhráithreacha Ailbhe Ó Monacháin,
Alfred Cotton, agus Bulmer Hobson*

Buíochas

Mo bhuíochas óm' chroí d'achan nduine a chuidigh liom agus an leabhrán seo idir lámha agam, go háirid: Alexander Archibald, Tomás Ó Monacháin, Maolsheachlainn Ó Caollaí, Jack Bennett, Séamus P. Ó Mórdha, Tom Barron, Jim Stevenson, Máire Nic Mhaoláin, Uilleam Mac Néill, Alf Mac Lochlainn, Aiken McClelland, Brendan Adams, Breandán Ó Buachalla, Pádraigín Ní Mhurchú, Art Ó Maolfabhail agus a bhean Máiréad, Mícheál Ó Cíosáin, S.P., Terence O'Brien, Charles Dickson, Jack McIvor, Liam Mac Reachtain, Proinsias Ó Conluain, Mgr. Tomás Ó Fiaich, Risteárd Mac Annraí, Roger Weatherup, Robert Cussen, Caitríona Nic Leoid, Gréagóir Ó Dúghaill, Séamus Mac Páirc, Adam Busby, Uilleam Mac Giolla Íosa, Cosslett Ó Cuinn, Seán Ua Cearnaigh, Rev. J.M. Barkley, Brian Ó Cuív, Éamon Ó Cuív, Risteárd Ó Glaisne, Bríd Dolan, Dr. R. Dudley Edwards, Theo J. Snoddy, Oonagh Warke, Mrs. C.V. Warke, Séamus Ó Saothraí, Aodán Mac Póilín, Seoirse Ó Luasa, Maolcholaim Scott, John Robb, Ruairí Ó Bléine, Seán Ó Cíobháin, Dr. A.P.W. Malcolmson, PRONI, Ciarán Ó Pronntaigh, Dr. Eull Dunlop, Cahal Dallat, Caomhín Mac Giolla Léith, Breandán Mac Suibhne.

Is tír gan tlacht, gan reacht, gan fhéile
Nach d-tuigeann treabh aon Máthar a chéile.

CONTENTS

Foreword

"Cé go bhfuil an stair in bhur n-éadan, bíonn meas mór againn go léir ar Phrotastúnach" [History may be against you, but we all have a great respect for a Protestant] said my friend Seán Ó Ríordáin, the poet, to me once. And Dr. Daly, Catholic Bishop of Ardagh and Clonmacnoise, has said that Ireland needs a genuine Protestant witness. Few seem to realise how much the Catholic Church is opening to Biblical and Reformation truth, or how far it has already gone in adopting not only Anglican but Puritan principles in worship.

Popular propaganda and racialist myth seems specially designed to prevent this witness from being either given or received. In spite of its falsity, it is generally taken for granted by the majority of our so-called Protestants and so-called nationalists. It generates fear which makes both factions a very *Magor missabib*—a terror round about, a terror to themselves and to their friends. According to this myth, we Protestant Irishmen are not Irishmen at all, but a foreign body of planters

11

and colonists. We are called up to retreat from one untenable position to another, to shut gates and build brass walls and die in the last ditch. We must all be ghettoised and *gleich-gestaltet,* and told how to vote and what to say. Apparently, we are to become manly and outspoken by talking only with those who agree with us! The weak-minded and large-mouthed individuals who expound these views are so busy attacking their fellow Protestants that they have no time for positive witness of any kind—supposing that they had any to give.

Fact, logic, and the very word of God are lost upon such deaf adders. One can but hope that there are still a few genuine Protestants left, who believe in Luther's doctrine of the freedom of a Christian man, and who will refuse to bow to any but God and resist attempts to organise or bully them. They will be prepared to speak out in the accent and language of the land in which they are rooted.

Superficial and unscrupulous persons have paid lip service to Irish culture and religion and made use of them without knowing anything about them or caring anything for them. Many of the present, and still more of the younger, generation are tempted to react by cynically—and equally superficially— depreciating and rejecting both, instead of examining them.

Mr. Pádraig Ó Snodaigh has himself pointed out to me that his surname is a planter one, disguised by Irish spelling, just as my own is a Gaelic one in a misshapen anglicised form. We owe him a great debt. He has been digging in our family graveyard, and has disinterred many interesting facts about our ancestors, which it is impossible either to refute or ignore. We are reminded that this Gaelic heritage is one which we share with the psalm-singing Sabbatarian Gael of the Highlands and Islands of Scotland, as well as with Irish Catholics of Saxon, Welsh and Norman ancestry. All of the Church of Ireland is reminded that three or four centuries ago we produced the first Gaelic Bible in days when Scottish Gaels were still reading and writing standard literary Irish (into which Calvin's *Catechism* and Knox's *Book of Common Order* were translated—and in which Mac Vurich composed his narrative of the wars of Montrose and the exploits of Alister Mac Donnell). We see also that Muiris Ó Droighneáin does not exaggerate when he tells us that "It was the Protestants who played the main part in language activities at the beginning of the 19th century" and observes that "it was a strange, unnatural sight when the Catholics began slowly and shyly to join in the work". He also points out (see his work in Irish on the *History of Modern Irish Literature*) that the Fenians officially—with a few exceptions— not only ignored, but discouraged that work.

Whatever our politics may be, we can surely afford to interest ourselves in what Kuno Meyer described as "the earliest vernacular literature in Europe" which began in the 6th century and came before Dante and his troubadours. Even the surviving spoken form of that language has been described by Robin Flower (head of the British Museum) as the most poetic vernacular in western Europe. I still remember from the one occasion when I met C.S. Lewis, seeing the flash in his eyes as he spoke of the two-thousand-year-old epic of Cuchulain, and what it ought to mean for an Ulsterman.

It is bad enough to try to saw off the branch on which you sit. But what are we to say of the suicidal nihilistic absurdity of trying to dig up and cut off our own roots? The old tree cannot survive transplantation. It is not yet so fruitless as to encumber the ground and to be fit only for cutting down. Like the rest of the Christian Church, it is in desperate need of a fresh rain of God's grace and spirit to fall like mercy from heaven which will make its growth and witness rich and fruitful.

Cosslett Quin

Derriaghy-born Reverend Canon Cosslett Quin is a retired Church of Ireland clergyman and was President of Oireachtas na Gaeilge in 1972 and 1973.

ONE

A Heritage Denied

> There was no country dancing. Long ago they had lost the arts of
> the ballad and the dance, which, as kin, they once shared with the
> ancient people of Ireland.

Thus Sam Hanna Bell's comment on the Ravara Fête in his
magisterial novel of Ulster life, *December Bride*.[1]

The musical union of Scotland and Ireland has, of course,
been commented upon often over the centuries. Giraldus
Cambrensis, for example, writing in the 12th century, said:

> It is to be observed however that both Scotland and Wales, the
> former from intercourse and affinity of blood, the latter from
> instruction derived from the Irish, exert themselves with the
> greatest emulation to rival Ireland in musical excellence.[2]

The harp was shared by highlands, lowlands and Ireland in
the 16th century[3], and commented upon then by Vincenzo
Galilei, father of Galileo.[4] Within Gaeldom the harpers moved

freely, whereas

> ... The English, aware of the importance of the poet-musician in
> Celtic society did their best to ridicule him, but in Scotland a
> visiting Irish musician had the right to expect better. Such a one
> was Rory Dall O'Cahan ... [who] came from Ireland and lived
> mostly in Scotland.[5]

Ó Catháin "was affronted" once by Lady Eglintoun
demanding "a tune somewhat peremptorily" and left the castle
in high dudgeon before being recalled, after "some fine
wheedling", and "in reconciliation he wrote 'Give Me Your
Hand'" which, of course, "has been a favourite with folk
musicians for many years ... in Scotland and Ireland".

Ó Catháin was said to have made such an impression at the
Scottish court that King "James called him over and rested his
hand on his shoulder", at which O'Caháin declared that "a
greater than King James has laid his hand on my shoulder"[6]. As
John Purser says, "It says a lot for James VI that he did not
rebuke the man when it turned out that the person supposed
to be greater than James was The O'Neill, a man far from
sympathetic to the cause of unionism which James set in
motion and worked for with such care."[7]

Ó Catháin "was only one of many Irish clarsairs to visit
Scotland". Much later, for example the Louth harper Eachlainn
Ó Catháin (1729-c.1790) was

> ... a regular visitor [and] is represented in the Scottish *Maclean-
> Clephane* manuscript which contains 36 harp tunes possibly collected
> before Bunting's work at the 1792 Belfast Harp Festival. Hempson,
> who played at that festival also visited Scotland

while Scottish harpers "studying in Ireland include Murdach
Mac Donald and Ruairidh Dall Morrison".[8] On one trip, Ó
Catháin was presented with Ruairí Dall Ó Catháin's harpkey by
Mac Donald of Skye.[9]

John Purser, whose study I am drawing on here, talks of

Scottish music being "its own" while so influenced by the shared language, over so much of its history:

> The earliest evidence for even slight divergence from the language shared by Scotland and Ireland is early sixteenth century"

that language and culture "of the Gaelic-speaking invaders" who absorbed that of the Picts.

That music, under which he finds a unity stretching from the Borders "to the Highlands with a Gaelic tradition stretching back at least 1500 years", was so akin to Ireland's that, he says, "with the Irish we have a traditional musical relationship which amounts to a shared identity".[10]

This point hardly needs to be stressed too much here—I doubt if there will be disagreement with Sam Hanna Bell on this point; the echoes resound in our ears.[11]

That all of us, however, share a very deep and very pervasive heritage in the Irish language is not well known: indeed it is often—too often—denied, ignored, objected to or opposed.

Another novel, Maurice Leitch's *The Liberty Lad* (Belfast, 1985 edn., p.73), in which Frank Glass's interjection of 'sláinte' in the Kildargan pub leads to

> ... a silence that told me I hadn't been included in the round. He probably put me down for a Papish into the bargain

points up the tragedy of that ignorance and hostility. To an extent this is understandable in the light of history: the 1831 National Education Act was designed, in the system it set up, to obliterate linguistic differences in Ireland and to eliminate almost completely the subject of Irish history from Irish schools.[12] That design was adhered to, as Dr. W.J.M. Starkie, the then Resident Commissioner of the Board of National Education, said in Belfast in 1902:

> his board, since its foundation seventy years previously, had waged open war on the Irish language.[13]

One of the results of this is a dangerous ignorance spreading into crude racialism—for example, in the claim that the plantations of the 17th century had led to a situation where "a certain preponderance of Celtic strain may be admitted for Southern Ireland, but certainly not for the North"[14]; something which a cursory knowledge of blood groups (should one need to go down that cul-de-sac of history) would have warned against trying out[15], something of which the fact that there was a larger proportion of Macs and Os in Belfast than in Dublin in, say, 1858 makes nonsense,[16] and something which was demonstrated as ludicrous by George Buchanan as far back as 1589![17]

Upon that ignorance, a version of a two-nations theory has in part been built. A divisive theorem[18], it is in a sense a recrudescence of something which was quite widely circulated about 80 years ago.[19] Used variously now by some of the more extreme unionists—it appeared on the 1994 European election literature of one of the smaller unionist parties for example—its present popularisation was initiated by the Stalinist[20] British and Irish Communist Organization in the early 1970s[21] and variants of it have been adopted by many on both sides of the border since then. Some of its advocates may be opportunistically or desperately clutching at the straw of an apparent short term 'solution' to the Irish problem. No such easy answer exists and to urge its existence is to do a great disservice to Ireland in time of crisis.

One common assumption is the assertion that the Irish language is not part of the 'heritage of the Irish Protestant community' and that this marks a historical linguistic divide between the 'two great communities inhabiting the island'.[22] The validity of that theory depends on a series of propositions which, upon examination, are not tenable. It depends, for example, on the equation of the six counties of Northern Ireland with Ulster, which (whatever may have constituted Ulster over the centuries) is simply not so. It depends on the separateness of the 'Ulster Protestant community' from the

Protestant communities in the rest of Ireland—but the very institutional forms of their largest churches are country-wide, as they have been since the Reformation became expressed in separate organisational institutional structures. It depends on the notion that the six 'planted' counties are those which now constitute the six counties of Northern Ireland, whereas Down, Antrim and Monaghan were the three Ulster counties not included in the Ulster Plantation. It depends on the belief that the 'planters' and natives never mixed socially or intermarried; and it does not take the presence of a UDA leader named Murphy and an IRA officer named Bell at the Lenadoon confrontation of July 1972, or any other set of counterpoints (Cosgrave/McCusker, Adams/Magennis, Fry/McGimpsey, say) to underline the fatuity of such an assertion—one can go back to Wilkinson's complaint that intermarriage, frequency of gossipred, and fosterage had led many of the English of the plantations into acceptance of the Irish ways and customs[23] or come forward to the observation of the Methodist Risteárd Ó Glaisne that:

> There has been far more intermarriage between Protestants and Roman Catholics down the centuries and right up to the present time than Protestants in their various denominations like to admit.[24]

As an aside, one might observe that differences can be—ought to be—exciting, challenging; contention creative; and may be and hopefully will be again. But in Ireland there is an overlay of recrimination, veiled and not so veiled accusations of treachery or self-advancement when property rights or inheritance (factors which caused transfer in the era of the Penal Laws)[25] are perceived as causes of change, when "there is still a belief among some Protestants that the Catholic Church teaches hatred of Protestantism'[26] It doesn't but its assertion of its being the One True Church could conceivably be so read. When the same Catholics are deemed to be not only non-Christians but followers of Anti-Christ (that is of Satan himself)[27] then contention can really wield a cutting edge.

But to return to the proposition that the Irish language marks a historic divide. It depends on the inference that the Protestant communities are uniquely the product of the plantation, that their missionary activity, attraction to their tenets or whatever, failed to draw thousands of the Irish-speaking indigenous population into membership—an idea that is insultingly arrogant in its blindness to fact. It depends finally, on the suggestion that the 'planters' were monoglot English speakers on arrival and that they so remained. 'Proof' by assertion is simple; the excavation of historical fact is much more difficult and certainty is an elusive quality in any historical examination. But such evidence as I hope to present will demonstrate the flimsiness of that final suggestion.

TWO

Languages of the Plantation

The pattern of developing events in Ulster did not depend on the Ulster Plantation alone, as the 1659 survey and census show. The population of Ulster then was returned as 103,923, of whom 63,272 were Irish and 40,651 were listed as 'English and Scotch'. In every county the Irish outnumbered the others, though in Tyrone and Antrim the differences were not so great.[1] Further, the survey shows that English (Scots was listed as English for the purposes of the survey[2]) was the majority language only in some towns, for example, Derry, Carrickfergus and Coleraine; East Donegal, the barony of Coleraine and the area between Lisburn and Larne.[3] Irish was the majority language everywhere else in Ulster.

Obviously, then, other factors were in operation. The patterns and the causes of the contraction of the Irish or Gaelic speaking areas throughout Ireland, Scotland and Man, the 18th century emigrations, the ten-fold multiplication of the population of Belfast in the 19th century and the often negative and hostile attitudes of churches and state to the various dialects of Gaelic over the centuries are some of the more striking agents in the language shift.

The Isle of Man is seldom referred to in these discussions but that Gaeldom once included Northumbria which is not adverted to either. An *Annals of Ulster* entry for 705 AD reads 'Aldfrith mac Ossu sapiens Rex Saxonum moritur'. Fergus Kelly adds "Flann Fína was the Irish name borne by the Northumbrian King Aldfrith son of Oswy, who ruled Northumbria from 685 to 705 AD. He had an Irish mother and studied in Ireland in his youth".(*A Guide to Early Irish Law*, Dublin, 1988, p.285) The same mother, by the way, used the calendar of the Celtic Church rather than that of Rome!

That aside, Man is an interesting example of a beneficial agent as regards the continuation of Irish (Man being 8.1 per cent Gaelic or Manx speaking as recently as 1901[4]). Manx immigration and the commerce of fishing contributed to the survival of Irish in Lecale[5], an area of mixed racial origin and ecclesiatical adherence.

A Franciscan priest of the Counter-reformation Aodh Mac Aingil (Aodh Mac Cathmhaoil, Hugh Campbell, Cavellus/ McAngell/Cavello) born near Downpatrick in 1571, studied in Man from 1589 to 1592 after spending the three years in a bardic school. In an undated but fairly recent study of Mac Aingil, Patrick Kearns cites Tomás Ó Cléirigh's suggestion that he probably attended Rushen Abbey there since the ruler was the Catholic 3rd Earl of Derby. The Act of 1539 for the suppression of the monasteries did not apply to Man, but Kearns adds that the Isle of Man lay within easy distance of the Down coast and

> ... Manx ... was a dialect of Gaelic which bore a close resemblence to that spoken in his native South-east Ulster, and ... Man in those days belonged to that Gaelic world which flourished still in Scotland and his native Ulster.[6]

Interestingly when Patrick Dunkin, Prebender of Dunsfort

in Co. Down in 1640, was "forced by three Puritan ministers to flee to the Isle of Man—which was both Gaelic-speaking and Royalist" he wrote a poem in Irish on his plight blaming "Roundhead thugs" for killing his people, destroying St. Patrick's faith and inventing a "religion without authority"— an echo of the prelacy versus presbytery disputations.[7]

The anti-nationalist colporteurs of the two nations theory assert that "except for a small Gaelic-speaking element", the language of "the people who came to Ulster in the immigration and plantation of the 17th century" was "Lowland Scottish, a form of English".[8] But the assertion about 'Lowland Scottish' is wrong on two counts. As regards the size of the 'Gaelic-speaking elements', the 1659 figures are an indication that it was very much larger than is often appreciated. (Other indications are given below.) But the non-Gaelic speakers comprised two quite separate groups—speakers of English and speakers of Scots.

English

The English speakers came from England and have left their mark on the English spoken in the central belt of Ulster extending east from Enniskillen almost as far as Belfast. This is called by dialectologists the 'Mid-Ulster Dialect' and its sources and extent have been mapped at the Ulster Dialect Archive, as has the 'North-Eastern Dialect', in which the phonological echoes of Scots are clearly heard.[9]

Scots

The Scots language mentioned here was often known in Scotland as Inglis, the term 'Scottis' being first used to describe it c.1520.[10] (Gaelic literature had been there for many hundreds of years beforehand.) Its roots and origin (being closest to Frisian among the Germanic languages) differ from those of Southern English—which was to become the standard English imposed from London outwards. H.J. Paton says:

> It is derived from the speech of the invading Angles who occupied
> the Lothians as well as what is now Northumberland.

whereas

> Southern English ... is a development of Mercian and has been
> dominated by London ... The Scottish speech is thus a form—in
> some ways an older form—of English or Anglish. It may be called
> a dialect of English (or if you prefer it, of Insular West Teutonic);
> but it is not, and never has been, a dialect of Southern English ...
> After the court moved to London in 1603 the old Inglis inevitably
> declined, but it survived—as Lallans—in the dialect of the people.[11]

Within living memory an interpreter had to be invoked to
translate the evidence of a witness whose 'Braid Scots' could
not be understood by the court in a legal case in Donegal. The
pressure towards Southern Standard English from the government in London and the neglect of the churches in teaching,
training or publishing in Scots (even if individual seceders like
Rev. Thomas Clark could "harangue God and man in
Kilmarnock bonnet and broad Scots" in Monaghan from 1751
to 1764[12]), have led to the situation where

> The days have long since gone when the Ulster poets like James Orr
> of Ballycarry could, in his *Irish Cottiers Death and Burial* (1817), write
> a poem more surely and consistently Scots than Burns's *The Cottar's
> Saturday Night*: when poets like Francis Boyle of Comber could
> write Scots verse which, in John Hewitt's words, 'seems to be the
> countryside itself articulate'.[13]

Irish

Church and state hindered the separate development of Scots.[14]
One Scot, Dr. Daniel Dewar (principal of Aberdeen University), spoke, after his 1812 visit, of there being

... In Ulster ... the three classes which divide Ireland—the native
Irish, the Anglo-Hibernian or English settlers and the Scots.

Though he strongly recommended teaching the Irish to read
the Bible in Irish he seems to have underestimated the extent
to which Irish had been or became a common language[15]. The
fact that there are "a small number of native Irish-speaking
members of the Church of Ireland in Donegal and Kerry"[16],
and that there were still Protestant Irish-speaking communities
of 'planter' origin in Ardara, Glencolmcille and Dunfanaghy
earlier in this century, are residual indicators of this.

Doubt has been expressed about the value of these indicators. One might advert to Dr. Leslie Lucas's reply to John
Bustard's comments on Irish when he said:

> Many Protestants in the Republic *do* spring from Gaelic roots. What
> about those having surnames such as McElhinny (my grandmoth-
> er's name), Gallagher, Doherty, Devenney, McGarvey, Dunlevey,
> etc. all of which exist in Co. Donegal? In addition to this, many of
> the Planter stock have Scottish Gaelic names such as McKinley,
> Campbell, McKinney, etc.
>
> In the old days many Protestants who were not of Gaelic stock
> spoke Irish; just the other day I was speaking to an old lady whose
> maiden name was Moore, and she remarked that her father was a
> native Irish speaker. In the last century, a cousin of my grandfa-
> ther's whose name was Wilkinson (surely a true Anglo-Saxon
> name) acted as interpreter for Irish-speaking litigants in the courts
> in Falcarragh.
>
> —*Irish Times*, 20th May 1994

An informant from Castlerock[17] avers that all the old people
in Dunfanaghy spoke Irish about 1930, and as regards Donegal
the fact that the man who headed the poll in the Donegal
constituency for the 1994 Údarás na Gaeltachta (Gaeltacht
Authority) elections was Dáithí Alcorn, a member of the
Church of Ireland, standing for Fianna Fáil, was a significant
recent indicator.

Danny Kennedy, an Ulster Unionist councillor in Newry has said his grandfather was an Irish speaker.[18] Dr. Bob Curran's grandfather from South Armagh was an Irish-speaking Protestant.[19] Christopher McGimpsey in saying that his forebears (O'Dempsey originally) lost "our native tongue" by the beginning of the 19th century, adds that for him his "interest in the language is more that of a homing pigeon returning to the roost than that of an outsider who has discovered something alien which attracts him".[20]

A major consideration to be borne in mind in dealing with the plantations and migrations in the 17th century is the extent to which the population movement from Scotland to Ulster was within what had been, and to an extent continued to be part of a single culture. That Irish had for long been the common language of Ireland, of most of Scotland and of Man must not be overlooked. Nor must the Ulster-Scottish kingdom of Dalriada from c. 480 to c. 700 AD, the Scottish united Gael and Pict kingdom founded under Gaelic leadership in 842 AD, the continued relationship with the kingdom of the Hebrides and Argyll (Earra Ghàidheal, 'coastland of the Gaels') from the 12th to the 16th century[21], the fact that the earls of Antrim are descended from Eoin Cathanach (so called because of his having been fostered with the Ó Catháin family in Ulster) the last of the kings of the Hebrides (a kingdom which came to an end in 1499 AD), the story of William Wallace from his redoubt in Selkirkshire (where Gaelic was spoken as late as 1931) raiding the linguistically-mixed northern counties of England in 1297 and using language as a factor of differentiation ('he spared no one who spoke the English tongue'), nor the 1315 letter from Robert Bruce to the chief men in Ireland offering alliance and recalling their common language, common custom and their one national ancestry.[22]

As Roger Blaney has pointed out, ecclesiastical evangelisation added to the Gaelicisation of Scotland, "so that at its height, the Gaelic language was spread over the entire area of Scotland". The evidence of placenames is such that the "results show clearly that Gaelic settlement, at one time or another ... included the whole of Scotland" and their "hegemony stretched so far as Cumbria and Northumberland".[23] The mercenary tradition of the 'Gallóglaigh' continued from the 13th to the 16th century and led to continued toing and froing between Ireland and Scotland.[24] This was to have its own echo in the activities of Randal Mac Donnell in the mid-17th Century:

> As half-chief and half-courtier (he was domesticised in the court at Whitehall and married the Duke of Buckingham's widow) with land and vassals on both sides of the Straits of Kintyre, Antrim's influence straddles all three Kingdoms. He played a provocative role in the earliest stirrings of the Irish-British crisis in the late 1630s ... [and] achieved his ambition [to make war on the Campbells] when a force he had raised ... left Waterford to join the Royalist forces led by Montrose in Scotland ... commanded by Alisdair Mac Colla—'Colkitto' to legend—they played a central role in the most amazing campaign in military history in these islands.

Some fought to the last with Montrose, the majority took "refuge in the Kintyre peninsula, where they were able to subsist among a population which included many of Antrim's vassals". Though under sentence of death, they were in effect exported as mercenaries to Spain![25]

Army movements and camp followers are often ignored in logging population shifts. Bruce, for instance, brought 6,000 with him in 1315.[26] When the loot and plunder of the retaken Newry and district was being divided up in May 1642, the English complained that the cattle had been spirited away "into the Ardes and Clandeboye" during the night. Munro, the Scottish general blamed "an infinite number of poor con-temptible countrymen which could not be reduced to order" for this. Mgr. O'Lavery says

> These were generally Irish native camp followers ... [who] settled down among their new friends, and from [whom] are descended

most of the Presbyterians who have old Irish names in the Ards, Castlereagh and Dufferin.[27]

In writing in Irish or Gaelic this cultural unity is most evident. The traditional bardic tour included both Ireland and Scotland. Hence the reference to Brian Mac Fhearghail Ó hUigín of Sligo (ob. 1476) being 'cend scoile Erenn ocus Alban' [head of the bardic order of Ireland and Scotland].[28] Another O'Higgins celebrating Sorley Boy Mac Donnell writes within that same unity[29], as did the Clan Ranald bards Cathal and Niall Mac Vurich (Mac Mhuireadhaigh)[30], some of whose work was edited for Conradh na Gaeilge by a Protestant author and Irish language revivalist, Seosamh Laoide, over eighty years ago.[31] As can be seen in their work there was little differences between both dialects.[32] The weakening tradition continued to stress the unity into the 18th century (see Tomás Ó Casaide's "Theighinn ó Oileán Mhic Aoidh go hAlbain Ghaedhealach" [I used to go from Islandmagee to the Gaeltacht of Scotland, c. 1750[33]] and even into the 19th—in the writings of the Islay poet Uilleam Mac Dhúin-Léibhe [William Livingstone].[34]

Early 19th century revivalists looked to this unity also, as the dedication to the Highland Societies of London and Edinburgh; the reference to the grammars of the Revs. Shaw and Stewart in Scotland; and these sentences from William Halliday's *Úraiceacht na Gaeidhilge: A Grammar of the Gaelic Language* (Dublin, 1808) demonstrate:

> It is to be fondly hoped the venerable and elegant Mother Tongue, the improved and written Gaelic of Ireland, will exhibit just claims to equal attention and admiration ... And as we are of common origin, let us labour in the common cause of reviving our common literature and re-erect the venerable fabric of its ancient importance.

The 17th-century plantation "brought for example Presbyterian Scots with names as familiar as McMenamin and Kennedy, who must be considered rather in the light of homing birds",

as one modern commentator puts it.[35] This echoes the suggestion of Sir James Hamilton in the Irish House of Commons, on
1st May 1615, that amity should subsist between both Scots and
Irish because of their common origin.[36] It echoes sentiments
such as these from the mid-18th century: "The Scots being
descended from the Irish*, or the Irish from them, no great
matter which; they are both but the same people, according to
the best historians"[37]. And it echoes an article by F.J. Bigger in
which he said: "When the Galloway planters came to Ulster
they were only returning to their old lands like emigrants
coming home again."[38]

In material culture, the unity has been noted also from the
statement about plantation society that its "... material culture
is strongly moulded to its Irish environment"[39], to Alan Gailey's
conclusion that:

> It is possible that the 17th century-planters were forced, to some
> degree, to accommodate themselves to an existing cultural-geo-
> graphical pattern, and that their advent to Ireland from culturally
> related areas ... meant that the plantation of Ulster as a whole was
> not so revolutionary as some historians have asserted, remember-
> ing that there were many settlers coming to Ulster also from
> culturally unrelated districts in England[40]

Again, Sheila St. Clair has stated that:

> Irish folkways know no geographical or political boundaries for

---

*"It is agreed on, by all Historians of any note, that the Scots are
descended from the Irish, the Irish being called Scots; from thence
came that Distinction of Great Scotland, or Ireland, and Little Scotland, or North-Britain. However, they are not agreed as to the time of
their first settling in Britain, for the Scotch Historians, viz. Hector
Boethius, Buchanan, Mackenzie say, that they settled there 300 years
before the birth of our saviour; and on the other hand, Usher, Loyd
and Stillingfleet affirm that they did not fix there till the Year of Our
Lord 503." (*loc. cit.*)

> though it was here in Ulster that I looked and learned ... their patterns with only the slightest variation at times are to be found all over Ireland, wherever songs are sung or stories are told.[41]

It has also been said that the Scottish Presbyterians who came to Ulster in the 17th century were mostly Gaelic speaking.[42] At least it is certain that the Gaelic-speaking element among them was a very large one, possibly the majority. Some indices of this have been adverted to above: more will be adduced below—in connection with the continuation of the use of Irish, despite, what was in the main, the hostility of the church and state establishments and despite the hostile attitudes of educationalists and consequent problems as regards, for example, literacy in Irish.

Attitudes to this problem must not be informed by the attenuated Gaeltacht of the present in Scotland and by this attenuation being projected backwards to the early 17th century. Nor must the plantation be seen as a once-for-all settlement affecting six counties. Before the main plantation those who were settled or who migrated were mostly Gaelic-speaking Scots.[43] The first Gaelic book in print was Seon Carsuel's translation of Knox's *Book of Common Order,* published in 1567, and the established church looked to Scotland for preachers in Gaelic for Ireland, as evidenced by Lord Deputy Sidney's suggestion of similiar nature to Queen Elizabeth in 1576, one paralleled by a recommendation to King James in 1604.[44] Traffic was not all one way, as the Irish Franciscan[45] and the Irish Vincentian[46] missions to parts of Gaelic-speaking Scotland in the 17th century demonstrate.

Sir Arthur Chichester "chief architect of the Plantation of Ulster"[47], and layer of the "rickety, even rotten, foundations"[48], of the present political edifice, was opposed to the bringing in of Scots:

> Chichester heard that the King was about to show his generosity in an especial manner to certain Scottish noblemen, to whom immense grants, it was said, were to be made, and who intended to

bring into Ulster large numbers of Islesmen and Highlanders as settlers. This naturally appeared to the Deputy a very questionable proceeding, for he had no special affection for Scotsmen, high or low, gentle or simple, and besides he had expended much of his time and ingenuity ever since his coming to Ireland, in the work of repelling and expelling Islesmen and other Northern Scots from the coasts of Ulster. He felt, however that his hands were now completely tied up by the accession of the Scottish King to the English throne and especially in view of an act to be passed at the meeting of the first Parliament in reference to this matter.[49]

His hands were in fact tied, by the repeal, in 1612, of an act from the reign of Philip and Mary "against bringing in Scots to Ireland, retaining them here, or intermarrying with them",[50] a repeal which followed the 1610 Act making the incoming Scots "denizens of both England and Ireland, thus securing their right of tenure to the lands allotted to them".[51]

Given the cultural unity which had obtained, and the movements of population over a thousand years between the north of Ireland and Scotland[52], and the number of Gaelic-speakers among the 17th-century arrivals, the plantation did not "do as much as might have been expected to lessen Scottish influence" on the Irish language in Ulster[53]. This factor may also, in part at least, account for the initial excepting of the Scots from the expulsion order of 1641[54], (during the aftermath of which there is a reference to Castlehaven not being able to understand Captain Fox's orders to his troops since they were in Irish).[55]

The Gaelic language was spoken over a much wider area of Scotland in the 17th century than is often realised. Galloway and Ayrshire, for example—areas from which many of the Scottish planters came—were to a considerable extent Gaelic-speaking.[56] It is said, for example, that the last recorded Gaelic speaker in Carrick (Ayrshire) died as late as 1760[57], but there is evidence of it lasting well beyond that date. It is known that old people spoke it in Glen Barr in 1820; that an elderly woman is noted as having been a Gaelic speaker in Ballantrae about

1830; and that Alexander Murray (1775-1813)—a herd's son from Kirkudbright and sometime Professor of Oriental Languages at Edinburgh University—had Gaelic as his first language.[58] Further, there was an advertisement for a teacher for Barr in 1762 which required a knowledge of Gaelic—which, given the fact that no teaching through or of Gaelic was then envisaged, can only mean that Gaelic was necessary so the teacher could communicate with the Gaelic-speaking children of the area.[59] Robert Louis Stevenson set his novel *Catriona* in Fife in 1752, taking it for granted that it was a Gaelic-speaking area and as late as 1705 there were sixty Gaelic-speaking families in Kirriemuir.[60] Highlanders had no difficulty in communicating with the inhabitants of 'Gallawa an Carrick' in 1715 and The '45, though they did have problems "wi the Eerish auxiliaries".[61] The Rev. J.C. Maitland referred to the use of Gaelic in Galloway around 1793.[62]

When one examines the origins of the planters one can only conclude that most of the Scottish ones (the English undertakers brought markedly fewer followers with them) must have come from Gaelic or bilingual areas. One more undertaker came from the west than from the east of Scotland (and the east was also partly Gaelic speaking then and this was true as far south as Berwick) and 26 of the lesser planters came from west of a line, drawn north/south, through Stirling, while twenty-one came from the east. This represented "a deliberate attempt to encourage westerners to participate at the expense of the easterners".[63] While this could have been because "planters from this part of the country would have less difficulty in transporting tenants and provisions to Ireland"[64], it is also possible that movement within related cultural areas was also a consideration, since, for example, there was only one planter from "the unruly Border areas"[65].

In 1610, the Scottish secretary of state wrote:

> ... the West cuntrey people of the common sorte do flock over in so greit nowmeris that muche landis ar lasting waste for lacke of tennentis.[66]

These soon "began to negotiate with the Irish, promising to intervene with the King on their behalf to permit them to retain their lands if, in return, they would supply either money or provisions".[67] Again mutual co-operation against the English was envisaged in the ill-starred 1615 plot of Mac Donnell, Ó Catháin, Ó Néill and William Stewart.[68]

The numbers who came were not regarded as satisfactory in 1621 when Sir Francis Blundell wrote that they were so few that "they will sooner grow wild with the Irish, than make the Irish Civill".[69] About 1630, the proportion of males in the escheated counties was 3 Irish to one immigrant.[70] It was then that the real flow began and large numbers came in from Scotland in the 1630s. Many of these came from what was then a Gaelic-speaking area. While the account may be an exaggeration, one

> ... English traveller, Sir William Brereton, was told in 1635 by a resident of Irvine, that, during the previous two years, 10,000 persons had passed through the town on their way to Ireland, having come from that part of Scotland lying between Aberdeen and Inverness.[71]

They were not the last of the Scottish migrants, since Gaelic-speaking episcopalians dissatisfied with the 1688 religious settlement drifted into north Antrim; "four or five hundred Hearers ... none of which understood English" from the Highlands were ministered to by two Church of Ireland clergy at their request after they had replaced the native Irish who had "left their habitations" after the Siege of Derry;[72] and they were succeeded by later groups of Gaelic speakers after 1715 and 1745.[73] Some of the descendants of these groups are known to have remained Gaelic speaking until the first half of the 19th century.[74]

Gaelic had been disparaged in Scotland after The '45 but, later on, the need for troops prevailed over prejudice, the pipe and the kilt were allowed and Gaels (even a son of Flora Mac Donald) joined the English army—so many that one writer commented on the fact that 20 Generals with little English, from the Scottish Gaeltacht, fought at Waterloo.[75]

Of greater relevance is the migration of Mac Neills from Kintyre, a group of Gaelic speakers who had embraced Presbyterianism "after the collapse of the McDonald cause in Kintyre". In Argyll, they stood up for Gaelic in church services, one of them supporting the publication of the psalms and short catechism in Gaelic and distributing Bedell's Bible (in Irish) in Kintyre. They forced the Lallans speakers to open their own kirk in Campbelltown! One, Niall, settled in Killoquin in Co. Antrim and John in Lower Faughart. Archibald and Malcolm settled around Ballymascanlon in 1688 and settled 30 to 40 families on their lands. The Mac Neills (later anglicised further to McNeale) formed by 1700 a congregation with a Gaelic speaker, John Wilson, as minister, until he resigned though retaining Carlingford and Narrow Water. He was replaced by Patrick Wilson who, in turn, was succeeded by the Rev. Mr. Drummond from Islay and he, in turn, was replaced by an Arran man, Colin Lindsay. The next two were Irish speakers from Belfast and Co. Down, Andrew Bryson (1786-1795) and Dr. William Neilson (1796-1818).[76] Of Neilson more anon.

THREE

The Irish Language
and Ulster Protestantism

Within the established church, there was a long and sometimes sharp debate on the use of Irish—even if over the centuries the bulk of the legislation was, with the state's, antipathetic. All the primates in the 18th century, for example, were English. Obviously English speakers picked up the Irish language "especially in areas where they were not so numerous"[1], as Brendan Adams has said, and many laws were enacted to counter the trend—with some legislation at least summarised in Irish (see the Earl of Ormond's response in Irish on behalf of the Lords and Commons of Ireland to the 1541 declaration of Henry VIII as King of Ireland).[2] In the south, we know that Spenser knew some Irish and that it was complained that "the English in Dublin do now all speak Irish".[3] Among the laws passed to reverse this trend was that of Edward IV in 1465 instructing every Irishman to take as surname the name of an English town, a colour, a trade or an office "under penalty of forfeiting his goods yearly". Similar legislation was imposed in Scotland.

Hence the number of Ulster surnames which hide a Gaelic origin.[4]

Such legislation was not in the short run successful, though in time and with other factors, the trend was reversed and English gained ground. One indication of Gaelicisation is the 16th century poem 'Litir Sheon Neilson Chum a Mhná', written apparently by an Englishman who lived about Dundalk and who had become attached to the court of O'Neill.[5]

Ambivalence was the order in the time of Queen Elizabeth; and her reign was marked by both trends. In 1551, Cranmer wrote to Cecil urging Turner of Canterbury for the vacant see of Armagh, hoping he would "take the pains to learn the Irish tongue ... then both his person and doctrine shall be more acceptable". (Turner refused.) Parliament a few years later urged the provision of ministers "who can speak English and who will reside", as well as the setting up of schools to teach English; while around 1569 preaching in Irish continued and the church obtained an order "setting apart in every principal town a church in which Divine Service might be conducted and a sermon preached in Irish". Though Elizabeth had an Irish primer and phrase book prepared for herself by the Baron of Devlin, and provided the first fount of Gaelic type in which such books as Kearney's *Catechism* (1571), the *New Testament* (1602) and the *Book of Common Prayer* (1608) were printed in Irish,[6] the Act of Uniformity in her era directed that the text of the *Book of Common Prayer* be in Latin for those without English.[7] Risteárd Ó Glaisne, himself a Methodist, has discussed

> ... the Church of Ireland's sense of an Irish continuity. It is proud to regard itself as the direct descendant of the earliest Irish Christians, and that has kept alive in the majority a very special feeling for Ireland ... [8]

Obviously that church was not dependent for membership on the Anglicans (mostly English) among the Planters—some of whom adapted themselves to the Catholic religion and were therefore free of the 1641 expulsions.[9]

Ó Buachalla, in his contributions to Pilib Mistéil's compilation *The Irish Language and the Unionist Tradition* (1994) suggests that, within Ulster, "the predominant process was one of continuity" especially as regards material culture and quotes in support this passage from Estyn Evans' 1973 book, *The Personality of Ireland*:

> ... the English planters soon gave up their half timbered houses—and adapted native styles. Similarily, agricultural implements, farming methods, domestic equipment, food, motor-habits, dialects, and many customs and superstitions, sooner or later took on an Irish flavour ... The great seasonal festivals of the pastoral years were taken over and the gale days (rent days) are neither English nor Scottish, but Old Irish, May 1st and November 1st ... The territorial arrangements of the land are substantially unchanged despite improving landlords; the little townlands with their predominantly Gaelic names, the smallholdings and tidy towns, the intimate network of roads or boréens serving the scattered farms and relict clachans. Paradoxically it is much-planted Ulster that has the highest proportion of Gaelic placenames among the four provinces.

Echoing Nicholas Canny, John McCavitt concurs: "British settlers initially became more acculturated to native Irish practice than vice versa."[10]

Events in Scotland were to have their effect on the Church of Ireland's policies and practices as regards the Irish language, many favouring its extirpation.[11]

There were, of course, Protestants in Ulster before the Plantation and, since they and their descendants are seldom adverted to, it may be pertinent to quote some data from Bishop George Montgomery when moving from Norwich to Ireland in 1605 to take charge of the dioceses of Raphoe, Derry and Clogher. Since he moved on again in 1610, and since the records included references to Hugh O'Neill, it is reasonable to take the report as being from the same period.

Not all of the names listed by Montgomery occur in Leslie's *Biographical Index* of the clergy of the Church of Ireland or in the typescript supplements in the RCB Library in Dublin. Among the clergy of Derry listed were John O'Henny (Henie), Rector of Banagher who knew Latin, Scots and Irish; Patrick M'Ready, Vicar of Camus, who was "learned in Irish and Latin"; Eugene McCawell, presented by the Crown in 1612 (Leslie) Herenach of Dunboe, "very learned after the manner of his people, especially in civil law, Latin and Irish"; Patrick O'Lynn of Tamlaghard "speaking Irish, Latin and English"; Eugene Mac Teggard, Rector of Cumber, "learned in Irish, Latin and English", who had two brothers who "speak English" (meaning, perhaps, that they had acquired it); William McTeggard, formerly Dean of Derry, "speaking Irish and Latin"; John McColgan, son of the rector of Donagh in Inishowen, "speaks Irish and Latin"; Hugh Donaldeus, Rector of Donaghmore and of Ardara, "clever in Irish, Latin and the Scots tongue"; Nelanus, brother of Hugh, a schoolmaster at Raphoe, "speaks Irish, English and Latin".

In Raphoe, he lists Terence O'Kelly (Turlough in Leslie, *op. cit.*) in Aughanunshin, "speaks Latin, Irish and English"; Bernard O'Gallagher, "commonly [known as] Brian Ounie Vicar of Tullyfern etc, ... speaks Irish, Latin and English"; James Crone "alias Shirrin, Rector of Clondevaddock [spoke] Irish [and] Latin"; "The same applies to Magonius McFadden in Mevagh; Donatus Maginnel "learned in Latin, Irish and Scots"; Nellanus McCallen "alias Groome ... speaks Irish, Latin and Scots"; Bernardus McNeilus "in Glencolumbkille paints cleverly and speaks Irish, Latin and English well, and is a curate"; Lodus Mc Swine "speaks Irish and Latin well"; "Of the same nature is ... Magonius McConnell ... and speaks Scots. Raymond O'Gallagher in Drumholm ..."; Roland and John Kengall "the sons of the late Bishop of Raphoe ... speak Irish, Latin and English".

In Clogher "The Archdeacon (James Duffe, according to Leslie, *op. cit.*,) speaks Irish and Latin"; Philip O'Dowie "in

Mucnoe speaks Latin (and) Irish" (Clogher Supplement, *loc. cit.*,); John McCardull "Vicar of Tydavnet speaks Irish and Latin", Tullius "his son ... studies at Drogheda"; The Dean of Lough Erne (whose name has not been located so far) "speaks Irish, Latin and English".[12]

Should similar visitation reports come to light the picture will be enlarged further.

Some of the bishops of the Church of Ireland were in favour of the use of Irish: Bishop Downham in Derry (1616-1633) for example; Donellan of Tuam (who was responsible for the translation and publication of the New Testament and the *Book of Common Prayer* in Irish in 1608 and 1602)[13]; Ram of Ferns; Rider of Killaloe and Wheeler of Ossory.[14] Elizabeth had "ordered, also, that services be conducted in Irish in one church in every diocese".[15] More than any one man it was the English born William Bedell who activated this policy—though opposed by primate Ussher who used his influence continually against the Irish language and towards rendering the Protestant establishment wholly English.[16]

That publication in Irish was deemed to be effective was reflected in the writing and activities of Aodh Mac Aingil who

> ... obviously believed that the Protestant publications were attracting Irish Catholics away from the old faith. No doubt this was not without foundation. Louvain would have been kept informed by friars stealing secretly into and out of Ireland as to the progress of the campaign of teaching Protestantism through the medium of Irish.[17]

Bedell, when Provost of Trinity College, arranged for prayers in Irish to be used in the chapel and that the Bible reading at dinner was also in Irish. He also insisted on instruction in Irish, especially for those who proposed to become clergymen, adding the practical "yearly stipend of £3" for each student "to help him in his study of Irish".[18] Consecrated Bishop of Kilmore and Ardagh at Drogheda in 1629, he then began to study Irish seriously, and two years later produced a bilingual broadsheet, *A.B.C. or the Institution of a Christian* (including the Lord's Prayer, the Decalogue, prayers and selections from the New Testament), specially prepared for the Roman Catholics of his diocese.[19] In 1632, he employed Muircheartach Ó Cionga (later Rector of Templefort) and William Nugent to begin the translation of the Old Testament into Irish[20], the major monument of the man who was to be called by his Irish neighbours 'Optimum Anglorum' (when given a military funeral by them), but which, after many vicissitudes, was not published until 1685. It was then published at the expense of the physicist and philosopher, Robert Boyle, who having had the New Testament in Irish reprinted, organised the editing of Bedell's Old Testament with the assistance of the convert from Catholicism, Andrew Sall, for publication and distribution in Ireland and Scotland.[21] In Scotland, it was used by Presbyterians until about 1830 and is the basis for the current Gaelic Bible.[22]

Against opposition from some of the landed gentry in his own diocese, Bedell had prayers read in Irish every Sunday in his cathedral and insisted on his clergy speaking, reading and writing Irish correctly.[23] The opposition came to the fore at the 1634 Convocation, but during it Canons 8, 86, and 94—dealing with the use of Irish, for example by a clerk reading in Irish "where the minister is an Englishman and (there are) many Irish in the parish" or the provision of books in Irish "where all or most of the people are Irish"—were enacted. Bedell more than anyone, though supported by the Archbishop of Armagh, was responsible for the victory of the pro-Irish party against Bramhall and others who asserted that his policy countered the interests of the state in that it opened too many doors to preferment for the "conquered and enslaved Irish".[24] A meeting of bishops in 1639 made further provision for the use of Irish in church services.[25]

The inter-regnum of Cromwell, as might be expected, disturbed the established church in its structure and organisation, and in its personnel. One who suffered was the Rev.

Patrick Dunkin, Prebendary of Dunsford, Co. Down in 1640, who, as we have already noted, was forced to flee to the Gaelic-speaking Isle of Man by three puritan reformers about the year 1650. There he composed the moving exile's lament 'Truagh Mo Thuras Ó Mo Thír', which Damien Ó Muirí describes as "B'fhéidir ... an dán is iontaí ón seachtú céad déag"[26] and about which Adams has written:

> When at this period a member of one Protestant church resorted to Gaelic verse for the purpose of chastising those of another Protestant denomination, it was certainly for no other reason but that Gaelic was his native tongue and that he had a sufficiently large audience of his own persuasion and language to make such poetic efforts worth while.[27]

After the restoration Dunkin returned to Ireland, where he is listed as Precentor of Armagh and Rector of Killeavy in 1666.[28]

In 1626, the Irish language was used "in common conversation and preaching in the Diocese of Armagh"[29] but throughout the 17th and 18th centuries—when exact information is hard to come by—along the east of Ireland in general the use of English was increasing, to a great extent because of educational policies and because of pressure from the civil administration.[30] Those pressures began to make themselves felt in the ecclesiastical administration also. While some bishops, Price for example, continued to promote the use of Irish,[31] and Huntingdon as Provost of Trinity College Dublin could urge in 1686 that "the Nation should make its language triumphant", nevertheless, others, Taylor, for example, the vice-chancellor of TCD at the time of Narcissus Marsh, were strongly opposed to the use of Irish.[32]

Marsh as Provost was in the Bedell mould and was firmly in favour of the teaching of Irish.[33] Parliament ignored a 1710 resolution from one of its committees for the provision of ministers capable of carrying on their ministry through Irish.[34] Ramoan and Culfeightrin Protestants had asked for Irish-speaking ministers about 1702, as did the Scotsmen in Rasharkin in 1690 "all comfortable Protestants" who could only speak Gaelic because of which "some of them were attending the ministrations of the Roman Catholic priest", and who, apparently, were denied service in Gaelic by their own Scottish clergy. This is probably the same group which Richardson refers to who, when "the Northern parts of the County of Antrim" were "deserted by the Irish, upon the landing of the English Army near Carrickfergus in 1689", settled there "in considerable numbers" and were ministered to as a result of representations by Duncan MacArthur first and later Archibald MacCollum.[35] The 1703 Convocation had before it proposals on the use of Irish; the pro-Irish resolutions in 1709 had not been resolved when convocation was prorogued; but further resolutions, in 1711, urging more translations into Irish had the result of a professor to teach Irish being appointed in TCD and of subscriptions being raised towards the training of preachers in Irish for Armagh and Derry Dioceses.[36] Of King, Bishop of Derry from 1691 to 1703 and powerful defender of the revolution of 1691, who had complained in 1711 about official opposition to preaching in Irish, it was said:

> ... he had indeed employed for a time, two Scottish Episcopalian ministers from the Highlands to preach in Irish in the barony of Ennishowen ... principally for the benefit of Highland Protestant families who had settled there after the revolution.

Another was similarly engaged in north Antrim.[37] In 1711 more printing in Irish for ecclesiastical purposes took place.[38] Though Dean Swift (who probably knew it) had regarded Irish as a nuisance to be got rid of[39], it did not disappear as readily as he wished: in 1758 a sermon in Irish was preached each day in St. Patrick's Cathedral, Dublin, during Passion Week.[40]

Though many lay Catholics had conformed—4,000 between 1703 and 1709, for example[41]—some clergy for 'Vicar of Bray' type motives, despite initial hopes that the Church of Ireland in Ulster would be served as far as possible by native clergy, bishops in Ireland were forced to look for clergy either in England or Scotland.[42] Many of the higher clergy scrambled for benefice and benefit rather than pastoral care—a scandal culminating, perhaps, in the career of the mostly absentee deist 'patriot Bishop' of Derry, the Earl of Bristol at the end of the 18th century.[43]

Another deist of Protestant background who knew Irish was John Toland of Inishowen.[44] Quite a different man was the Dungiven born James Mac Sparran (M. A. Glasgow 1707, ob. USA 1757) author of *America Disaffected*, an Irish speaker who preached frequently in Irish.[45]

Not all of the civil administration followed the Dublin lead in despising Irish, and among those who knew Irish there were some who were patrons of Irish writers. One of the Brownlows of Armagh was sometime patron of Peadar Ó Doirnín, probably the most celebrated northern Irish poet of his time. Ó Doirnín's mother, according to some accounts, was a Protestant.[46] Arthur Brownlow (MP, 1692-1699 and 1703-1710) knew Irish, as is attested by a colophon in his own hand on a collection of bardic verse (which had been written at the end of the 17th century for the head of the O'Neill Clannaboye family, and which later passed into the possession of Lord Moira, a descendant of Arthur Brownlow, who had it in 1765)[47] and by his translation into English of an elegy on the death of Eoghan Rua Ó Néill.[48]

He was even more interesting than that, however. He was a Chamberlain on his father's side and a descendant of Sir Seán Óg Ó Dochartaigh of Inishowen on his mother's. When Flann Mac Maoir, the last hereditary keeper of the *Book of Armagh* (one of the native Irish to give evidence against St. Oliver Plunkett, who was half hanged, drawn by hurdle and dismembered as a result) was going to London for the purposes, he pledged the manuscript for £5 to meet the expenses and it was thus that it was preserved. As Ó Buachalla says: "It is indeed a curious, ironic and not insignificant twist of history that the famous *Book of Armagh* should be sold for a pittance by its hereditary custodian and purchased in its turn by a representative of the new land-owning class."

Brownlow had more Irish manuscripts than that:

> Lhuyd in his *Archeologica Britannica* lists twelve Irish manuscripts then [end of the 17th century] in Brownlow's possession; he was patron of Eoghan Mac Oghannain, the main Irish scribe in southeast Ulster in the last quarter of the 17th century.[49]

Brendan Adams has suggested that this

> ... patronage of Irish by the principal landlord of this area may have delayed here the rate at which Irish speakers became bilingual in the late seventeenth and eighteenth centuries and this in turn may have delayed the rate at which their bilingual descendants in the late eighteenth and nineteenth centuries finally abandoned the use of Irish.[50]

Ó Buachalla adds the rider:

> That the High Sheriff of County Armagh and one of the principal landowners in the county should interest himself in Irish literature is in itself revealing and interesting: more significant, however, are its implications for any comprehensive sociocultural analysis of post-Plantation Ulster. It suggests that the simplistic monolithic view of life in Ulster usually presented to us by our politicians (one in which all natives are Catholic Gaelic and Republican and all Planters are Protestant, English and Loyalist) does not stand up to objective scrutiny, and that the three allegiances which people ascribed to—religious, political and cultural were neither synonymous nor identical; in particular cultural allegiance cut across social, political and religious alignments in Ulster.[51]

In a lecture in 1973, Ó Buachalla "indicated that lists of Protestants prominent in church life and on juries in Ulster at an early stage showed a greater number of Gaelic than of English surnames".[52] We are only beginning to understand!

On the spiritual side the first known translation into Irish of the *Imitatio Christi* (or portion of it) was commissioned by the Irish-speaking Rev. Nicholas Browne, who ministered in Fermanagh and Tyrone between the years 1704 and 1710.[53] In 1722, a special catechism was printed in Belfast, in Irish for the benefit of the people of Rathlin.[54] In 1711, Rev. John Richardson (sometime Rector of Belturbet) published a translation into Irish of a small volume of English sermons.[55]

Manuscript D3577/1A in the Public Record Office of Northern Ireland is a copy of the book printed by James Blow in Belfast, part of which is in the hand of Dr. Francis Hutchinson, Bishop of Down and Connor. (The rest is probably that of Archibald Mac Collum.)

Richardson, to whom Bishop Hutchinson wrote in 1721 about his translation of the Book of Common Prayer into Irish[56] was beneficed initially in Tyrone before moving to Belturbet in 1709[57]; had as well as the Book of Common Prayer, a catechism, five sermons and a promotional tract of his own printed[58], and lobbied widely until deemed a crank, for further use of Irish, including Swift among his targets.[59] He was, in Barnard's view, the end of a disputation within the church whether to use English or Irish. Where Bishop Dopping had introduced a bill in 1697 to ban Irish, Richardson promoted its use "because the Irish, once converted ... would forsake their distinctive customs, including their language". Bishop King, ultimately more pro-Irish than Richardson

... first as Bishop of Derry and more recently as Archbishop preferred Irish speakers to livings conscious, especially in Derry, that the greedy Presbyterians nibbling and sometimes gobbling Church of Ireland congregations, used Irish where it was needed. [He] wanted the Irish Church to fill a third of its benefices with Gaelic speakers, and pointed to Wales to show what a more enlightened language policy could do.[60]

But that phase ended, in Barnard's view (although he too seems to underestimate the number of Irish-speaking Anglicans who would expect services in their own language), with:

> The Established Church, meanwhile, [leaving] it to individuals, if they could, to obey its canons and preach or minister in Irish ... [61]

A newly aggressive policy of teaching through English, impelled by Bishop Maule and General Robert Stearne[62], led to a situation where:

> The new faith in this approach coupled with the related (though disputed) decline in monoglot Irish speaking, best suggest why, between 1722 and 1790s, the Church of Ireland did little to evangelise in Gaelic.[63]

Except for the Franciscans, the Irish Catholic attitude to Irish was unclear, uncertain and unfocussed for most of the same period.

To add to the picture of intermingling, a recent publication on 1641 has shown that

> Gaelic and Old English families were linked by blood and marriage to noble and aristocratic families in Scotland and England. Centuries of intermarriage and alliances created tenuous links of all kinds between the more powerful families in the three centuries. *Leabhar Cloinne Aodha Buidhe*—the book of the O'Neills of Clandeboye (Lower)—contains poems for Sir Henry (son of Sir Seán Mac Brian) O'Neill [d. 1638], and his wife Martha Stafford ... an English woman, and a Protestant. Sir Henry O'Neill himself may have been reared a Protestant. Poets such as Fear Flatha Ó Gnímh and Gofraidh Mac Briain Óig Mic an Bhaird wrote poems for Sir Henry ... and ... his wife ... without adverse comment on either her race or religion ... In support of the marriage the poets list the heroes of the history of the Gael, whose wives and mothers came from the nobility or royalty of England ... in an area as tense as Lower Clandeboye [south-east Antrim in this period], where several layers of settlers and planters jostled for position and possession, the poets ... evinced neither sectarian preoccupations nor xenophobia.[64]

And this was not only 'upstairs', as another commentator in

the same volume demonstrates:

> In the years before 1640 most settlers had reached local accommodation with the native Irish. At the upper social levels many native Irish had accepted positions in local and central government (he lists Sir Phelim O'Neill, Philip O'Reilly and Rory Maguire) ... At the lower social levels there is also evidence of ties of intermarriage, trust as evidenced by bonds of debt, and landholding between native and newcomer. William Skelton, one of Sir Phelim's tenants at Kinnard, deposed that before the rising natives and newcomers "differed not in anything ... save only that the Irish went to mass and the English to the protestant church" ... Richard Bellings ... (rather naïvely) felt that "the colonies (setting aside their different tenets in matters of religion) were as perfectly incorporated and firmly knit as frequent marriages, daily ties of hospitality and the mutual bond between landlord and tenant could unite people".[65]

Non-Conformists

In a letter to Richardson published, in 1711[66], one J. Maguire, sometime surveyor of forfeited estates, particularly in Co. Antrim, said:

> I met many of the inhabitants, especially of the Baronies of Glenarm, Dunluce and Killconway, who could not speak the English tongue; and asking them in Irish what religion they professed, they answered they were Presbyterians, upon which I asked them further, how they could understand their minister preaching; to that they answered, he always preached in Irish ... His audience ... was composed of native Irish and Highlanders.

Richardson cited another correspondent, Archibald Stewart, who said that a dissenter, also named Stewart, "by preaching in Irish [in North Antrim] has brought over a considerable number of Irish to be his hearers".[67] The Rev. Humphrey Thompson, first minister (1698) of the 1st Ballybay, preached on alternate Sundays in English and Irish.[68]

McSkimmin says a form of Gaelic was spoken in the Scotch Quarter in Castlefergus until about 1800, which local Irish speakers found difficult.[69] Perhaps it was more akin to the differing Gaelic of Scotland which Brendan Adams suggests formed the basis of the Irish of Red Bay[70], but however strong the pressure to shift languages was the survival of Irish among Presbyterians was more tenacious and longer lasting than is often accepted.

Archibald Mc Sparran, who was reared near Dungiven before emigrating around 1786 to Philadelphia, had his *Irish Legend of McDonnell and the Norman De Borgos* published in Belfast in 1829 and in it "one finds Gaelic phrases still current in his time".[71] The Rev. James McGregor, born near Magilligan in 1677, was a preacher in Irish and emigrated to America with part of his congregation in 1718.[72]

America poses an interesting and possibly important source of further enquiry. Luke Gardiner (later Lord Mountjoy) said in 1784 that one half of Washington's army spoke Irish.[73] Commenting on this Eoin Mac Neill once said:

> These must have been Catholic immigrants in the main, but not all, for Irish was spoken by many of the Presbyterians of Down and Antrim, was in fact their ancestral tongue in Cantire and Galloway.[74]

Mac Neill goes on to say (incorrectly) that, for the most part, the Presbyterians spoke English with more or less of "a Scotch dialect". But the sums don't add up. A total of 40,000 people were said to have emigrated from Ireland to America in the 40 years before 1773.[75] In 1785, Fr. (later Bishop) John Carroll computed the total Catholic population in the colonies as 26,000, of whom little more than half were Irish.[76] Now, that 26,000 were not all male either! According to Washington's Secretary of War, Knox, the strength of the Continental Army was 27,443 in 1775; 46,891 in 1776; 34,820 in 1777; 32,899 in 1778; 27,899 in 1779; 21,105 in 1780; 13,476 in 1783. One must bear in mind also that the Irish were split in loyalty (as all groups were) and many enrolled on the loyalist side. One such loyalist unit was the 105th Regiment of Foot, the Volunteers of Ireland, according to Grattan Flood, "had a band of Irish warpipes".[77]

If Luke Gardiner was correct, the bulk of the Irish-speaking soldiers in Washington's army must have been Irish Presbyterians since we know that they, more than Irish Catholics or Irish Anglicans, comprised most of the Irish emigration west in that period.

In 1710, the Belfast synod of the Presbyterian Community, extending from the 17th century examples of Rev. Jeremiah O'Quinn and Rev. Gabriel Cornwall in Billy, Co. Antrim, sent six ministers and three probationers to preach in Irish (McClean of Markethill, Thompson of Ballybay, McGregor of Aghadoey, Dunlop of Letterkenny, Wilson of Carlingford, Boyd of Maghera, Higginbotham of Coleraine, Plunkett of Glasslough and Dunlop of Derg) presumably to the Roman Catholic community.[78] They also arranged that congregations who wanted Irish-speaking ministers "are to exchange members with those who can speak Irish"[79], within the community.

It was said that as "late as 1716 ten per cent of the Presbyterian clergymen in Ulster could speak and preach in Irish, of whom one was Rev. Patrick Plunkett of Glennan, grandfather of the famous William Conyngham, first Lord Plunkett and another Archibald Maclaine, whose son Thomas was ordained minister in Monaghan in 1718".[80] In 1717, the numbers of Irish-speaking ministers in Ulster was increased by three ministers and three probationers.[81] It was also arranged to set up a school in Dundalk for the teaching of Irish in order to equip these ministers properly, and to have a catechism printed in Irish.[82] The Rev. John Wilson was in charge of the Dundalk school at first, but, quite early on, the Rev. Patrick Simpson, a Scot from Islay in Argyllshire, was put in charge. He in turn produced a small grammar and catechism in Irish.[83]

Simpson's workload was heavy. In 1716, the synod ordered "that Mr. Patrick Simpson preach in Dublin in the Irish language for the space of three months, he returning every month to supply his own congregation one Lord's Day during his absence". In 1717, he was again ordered to Dublin for three months in response to a memorial "with respect to the supplying of the Highlanders and Irish in Dublin, and thereabouts, with preaching in their own language" (this at a time when Capt. O'Neill was looking for probationers in Argyllshire "qualified for preaching in Irish").[84] Simpson himself was to look "for a gentleman that can preach in the Irish language" as an assistant, much later on, about 1765.[85]

In 1717, the tour of duty of the other preachers had McClean in Benburb, Dungannon, Cookstown, Minterburn, Monaghan and Stewartstown; McGregor in Derry, Antrim and Tyrone; Dunlop in Donegal; while one of the new men "The Rev. John Abernathy of Antrim exhibited great zeal in the work".[86]

From the *Fasti* we can list the following Irish-speaking ministers of the period, some of whom we have already encountered: John Wilson in Ballymascanlon, born in Scotland in 1667; Robert Stewart born near Carland, who worked with the Tyrone Presbytery 1716; Thomas Strawbridge from Burt who was licensed by the Derry Presbytery in 1717 and ordained at Carndonagh in 1721; Andrew Bryson from Belfast, who worked in Bangor and Dundalk; William Neilson; Samuel Delap (or Dunlop) of Ballyshannon, licensed by Derry 1706, ordained in Letterkenny in 1707; John Dunlop (or Delap), another Donegal man, licensed in Convoy in 1706, ordained in Donegal in 1710; Robert Higginbotham, an Antrim man, licensed in Antrim and ordained in Coleraine 1710, who later ministered in Killyleagh and Derry. His daughter married another Higginbotham, the Rev. Thomas of Pettigo; Samuel Irwin of Killeshandra, licensed in Monaghan in 1716, ordained in Lislooney in 1718; James Glendinning, a Scot born in 1583, ministered at Coole (or Carnmoney) Carrickfergus and Oldstone (Muckamore), before returning to Scotland; Charles Lynd of Rathmullan, licensed in Convoy in 1706, ordained in Clandevaddock (Fannet and Rathmullan) in 1708 and minis-

tering in Coleraine around 1728; James McGregor who emigrated to America with part of his flock; Archibald Maclaine of
Argyll, who came to Ireland and was installed in Markethill in
1700. Considered one of the best masters of the Irish language
in his day, he had four sons, the Revs. Daniel (Arran), Thomas
(Monaghan), Archibald (Banbridge) and Alexander
(Ballynahinch and Antrim); James Plunkett, a convert from
Catholicism from Cairncastle, was licensed in Antrim and
ordained at Glennan in 1714—his son, the Rev. Thomas
ministered in Enniskillen and later in Dublin; Patrick Simpson
from Islay, another of those who ministered in the Irish-
speaking Presbyterian community in and around
Ballymascanlon and Dundalk; Humphrey Thompson, who was
ordained at Ballybay, and Robert Thompson, who was ordained at Belturbet in 1713.

Despite the trends and forces impelling them otherwise, the
Presbyterian communion continued to be exercised by the
question of the priority of using Irish. So too was the established church as can be seen in many of Berkeley's *Queries*[87],
this one, for example: "Whether there be any instance of a
people being converted in a Christian sense, otherwise than by
preaching to them and instructing them in their own language." The Presbyterian interest and tradition continued in
such figures as the Rev. James Bryson (Lisburn, 1764-1773,
Rosemary Street, Belfast, 1773-1792, and Donegall Street,
Belfast, 1792-1796), who was an Irish-speaker, and father of
Samuel and Andrew; and David Fullerton of Ballymena 1755
and Carrickfergus 1756.[88]

While some of the Irish-speaking Protestant clergy were
occupied in missions to Roman Catholics, others were minis-
tering to their own communities—for the first 30 years of the
19th century Irish was still the home language of a great part
of Ulster.[89] The religiously-mixed area of Coroneary was bilingual throughout at the end of the 18th century.[90] One of the
first women preachers we have records of, a Quaker from near
Coleraine, Katherine Norton (*née* McLoughlin), is noted as
preaching in Irish in the Protestant town of Lurgan in 1678.

Her brother, Domhnall, was Rector of Clonmany parish, north of Derry, in 1672 while another brother was a parish priest![91] "Native Irish-speakers, followers of John Wesley—men like Charles Graham, Gideon Ouseley and Tomás Breatnach— evangelised in Irish".[92] The Rev. William Laing, a native of Perth, preached in Irish in the Newry district from 1780 to 1816, and was also called on to preach in Irish to the Presbyterian settlers about Ballymascanlon in County Louth.[93]

A factor often overlooked in discussions of language and religion is the number who changed. As Ó Buachalla has rhetorically asked: "How does one explain the fact that a large proportion of the surnames in the first Presbyterian congregations in Ulster were Irish?"[94]

Séamus Ó Saothraí has written about a few of those "Gaeil a chuaigh le Preispitéireachas". The first in the series was the Rev. Patrick Plunkett.[95] Another was the Rev. Jeremiah O'Quinn "patronised by Arthur Upton of Castle Upton, the proprietor of Templepatrick, who, with a view to his becoming a teacher to the Gaelic-speaking population, sent him to Glasgow University". He ministered in Athy and parts of Connacht before returning to Billy.[96] The third in his series was no clergyman but Col. Owen O'Connolly who leaked the news of an impending rising in 1641, but was not taken seriously enough. He later joined the Cromwellian 'independents'[97]. Next was the Rev. Michael Brannigan from Tyrone, who died 1874 after long service in the Presbyterian Irish-medium schools.[98] The last two were the Rev. George S. Keegan of Scotch Quarter, Clontibret, who ministered in Mayo and died in 1890, and Patrick McMenamy from Magherafelt, who was in the Glens of Antrim before emigrating to America.[99]

Closer examination of synod voters and jury lists may reveal more congruence. Roger Blayney, in disagreeing with Mac Neill and others, shows that English was not the language of the early Presbyterians in Ireland. He lists them in language order as:

Irish-speaking converts
Speakers of Scots Gaelic
Those who had learned Irish
Speakers of Lallans (Scots)[100]

Some would have been bilingual or even trilingual in time and, of course, the first three categories overlap in mutual and facile comprehension.

A further section from Blayney, drawing on Adams's pioneering study ('Aspects of Monoglottism in Ulster', *Ulster Folklife*, Vol. 22, 1976), is given here based as it is on the most recent and thorough examination of the available sources:

> Another significant influx into the pool of Irish-speaking Presbyterians was the substantial rate of conversions from the native Irish. The extent of this element has been underestimated. Latimer edited the old Session Book of Templepatrick Presbyterian Church, Co. Antrim and remarked on the number of members of the congregation who bore purely Irish names. The book covered the period 1646 to 1744, and some of the names noted were; Murdock O Donnallie, Oyen McGouckin, Jein McGee, Meive O Conalie, Patrick O Mory, Schilie O Donaly, Shan O Hagain, Donald O Crilie, Rorie O Crilie Jenkin O Conally. In a footnote Latimer was moved to say:

>> The number of Celtic names which occur in this record is remarkable. How have these names disappeared from among the northern Irish Presbyterians? In all probability they have become anglicised. If this has taken place even in districts where the Celts live together in large bodies, much more will it take place where they are a minority among the 'Scots'.

> Looking for the contemporary names of ministers and elders in a sample of modern congregational histories, one can note a very large number of purely Irish names, such as Grogan, McDermott, Hempsey, Callaghan, Roddy, Hegarty, Lavery, McGladdery, Shannon, Coyle, Megaw, Farley, Murphy, McBride and Drennan. The most noticeable characteristic, however, is the absence of the

prefix 'O', which means a descendant. Conversely, 'Mc' (Mac, meaning *son*) is exceptionally common. In order to conform to the stereotype that all Presbyterians came from Scotland, a first step would be to drop the 'O'. As suggested by Latimer, there were certainly further steps towards anglicisation. Some apparently English surnames were used to replace the native form. While some substitutes chosen seemed completely random—Houston for Mac an tSeachlainn (Mc An Taghlen), and Englishby for Mac an Gallóglaigh (Gallogly)—yet most name changes had some rationale. Mac an Rí (McAree) became King; Mac Ruairí (McRory) became Rogers; Ó Loinsigh (Lynch) became Lindsay; Ó Baoill (Boyle) became Boal; Mac Seáin (McShane) became Johnston. So, many apparently English surnames can hide the origins of their bearers—Armstrong, Baird, Smith, Cromie, Howard, Lambe, Woods, Haire, to name but a few.

Adams carried out a detailed study of one particular congregation, Saintfield First Presbyterian Church, which was founded in 1658, and still uses the old Irish name of Tonaghneave (from Tamhnach Naomh). He found an extensive list of members of the congregation bearing old Irish surnames, such as Kelly (Ó Ceallaigh), Connolly (Ó Conghaile), Kinghan (Ó Cuinneáin), Downey (Ó Maoldomhnaigh), Dornan (Ó Dornáin) and Flynn (Ó Floinn). He also pointed out that many other persons could have had their Irish surnames subsumed under more English sounding names.

This means that, to measure the extent of historic recruitment to Presbyterianism from the native Irish, one could not depend on a modern count of Irish surnames. Such a count would grossly underestimate the trend.

The substantial number of early Presbyterians who spoke Irish because they were native Irish would naturally lead to increased intermarriage and further spread of Irish throughout congregations.

Because Irish was the prevalent tongue and because very many people did not understand English, the newcomers who were not Gaelic-speaking would, of necessity, have to learn some in order to converse with the public, for purposes of trade and employment. Others would look on the acquisition of the language as an added dimension to their lives and a way of making contact with a wider community. Later again, many came to hold Irish literature and song in high regard, and made positive efforts to save and promote the language for its own sake.

The language groups among the early Presbyterians, therefore, would have been:

1. Irish-speaking converts
2. Speakers of Scots Gaelic
3. Those who had learned Irish
4. Speakers of Lallans (Scots)

Not many in any of these groups would have a facility with English ... The Irish-speaking converts, who were so plentiful, would have continued speaking Irish early into the 18th century, because, as Adams commented:

> One can change one's religion in a year or two, but it takes a generation or two to change a family's language.

The Presbyterian community in Ballymascanlon and Dundalk was settled, as we know, by the MacNeill brothers who, though bilingual (Gaelic and Scots), ensured that the language of ministry was Irish. Tolerant in practice, the Catholic primate in the late 1730s lived on their lands under the pseudonym of Dr. Ennis and held a congress of his clergy there in 1744.[101] Pádraig Ó Pronntaigh (he of the more celebrated Brontë family), Irish scribe and poet, lived at Ballymascanlon at this time. Beití Mac Néill, daughter of Malcolm, had a song written for her by O'Carolan. Four of Andrew Bryson's sermons in Irish have survived in the Bryson-MacAdam Collection in Belfast.[102] Andrew was one of their ministers.

The London Hibernian Society, founded in 1806, had as its object the teaching of pupils to read the scriptures in Irish or English.[103] The Rev. Robert Allen of Stewartstown superintended the setting up of their schools and soon he claimed to have 30 schools with 1,400 pupils learning to read the Bible in Irish. In 1840, there were 98 of these schools in Tyrone, 25 in Antrim, 16 in Galway and 20 in Mayo. By 1845, it was claimed—

a disputed claim—that over 17,000 adults had been taught to read Irish in these schools.[104] Publishing in Irish had to keep pace with this development. In 1816, the Irish Quaker Tract Association issued 2,000 copies of the Sermon on the Mount in Irish[105], the British and Foreign Bible Society produced the entire Bible in Irish in 1827[106], and the Presbyterians completed an Irish metrical version of the Psalms on the advice of Dr. Norman MacLeod in 1836.[107] The Achill Mission and Press, which produced an Irish Grammar, was guided by a Dublin-born native-Irish speaker, Rev. Edward Nagle.[108] Another missionary group of that period was the Society for the Promotion of the Education of the Native Irish through the Medium of their Own Language.[109]

One of the more colourful characters of this period was the Rev. William Neilson, ordained in Dundalk in 1799. He opened a school there which was "attended by all denominations and from it has students sent for TCD, Maynooth, and the Scotch Universities". In 1808, he published his 207-page *Introduction to the Irish Language* and followed it up with *Céad Leabhar na Gaoidheilge*, which was, it is claimed, "the first elementary class book prepared and published in the Irish language".[110] He preached regularly in Irish and was once arrested by the yeomanry for so doing in Rademon. There is a notice in the *Newry Telegraph* of 1st June, 1813, announcing his intention of preaching in Irish in the Presbyterian meeting house there on the 4th. The editor added: "To those who are proficient in Irish or who have made some progress in learning that language, the discourse of the learned doctor will be a source of much gratification and improvement"[111]. In the preface to his *Introduction* Neilson wrote:

> In this language are preserved the remarkable annals of our country ... It has been said, indeed that the use of this language should be abolished and the English prevail universally ... it is surely reasonable and desirable that every person should be able to hold converse with his countrymen as well as to taste and admire the beauties of one of the most expressive, philosophically accurate

and polished languages that has ever existed.[112]

Neilson was the son of the Rev. Moses of Castlederg who came to minister at Rademon, near Crossgar. He used Irish, it being said of him in 1784 that "the Dissenters and Papists of the parish mostly speak in that language, and his prayers and discourses are made in it".[113] In 1769, he began the grammar of Irish completed by William. Another son, Arthur, was one of the non-subscribing ministers who withdrew to form the Remonstrant Synod. Moses opened an academy in Rademon which, in addition to sons of his own congregation "prepared young men intended for the Catholic priesthood in Latin, Greek ..."[114] His son James's academy in Downpatrick was similarily open and three Catholic bishops of Down and Connor were trained there. The fourth son, William the grammarian, had a similar school in Dundalk.[115] They were, of course, functioning within a vibrant Irish-speaking community.

Baptist Society schools from 1814 were also teaching "the Irish peasant to read the Bible, if necessary in his own language", but this was mostly in Munster and Connaught.[116]

Local records, the history of the not-celebrated, so to speak, contain much that is relevant. For example, in 1814 the Rev. William McGhee, Rector of Upper Badoney in Tyrone said: "English and Irish are spoken in common by Protestants and Catholics ... We all carry well together, no party business, we have neither orange nor ribbon men"[117].

The Presbyterian Ernest Blythe (born 1889) mentioned an Irish-speaking relative of his mother's from South Down[118]; "The Rev. Mr. White introduced (O'Donovan) to a Presbyterian who thought he knew Irish" in Rathfriland in 1834[119]; Aodh de Blácam, in the 1934 article already mentioned, says that

> ... as recently as the youth of the present writer's father, Protestants in Newry (an industrial Ulster town where complete anglicisation might be expected) talked Irish to the incoming country folk on market days, and many were proud of whatever Gaelic they knew—

few seemed to have regarded it as 'not theirs' ...[120]

Denis Ireland wrote about his maternal grandfather, James McKnight of Rathfriland:

> Actually he was a Presbyterian minister and somewhere about the middle of the last century he preached from the pulpit of a small Presbyterian church in County Louth in English in one Sunday, in Irish the next.[121]

Dr. James McKnight's father was a farmer in the Rathfriland area and an Irish speaker himself. James was a leader of the tenant right movement in Ulster. When he was dying in Derry he asked an old Catholic servant to repeat the Lord's Prayer in Irish to him.[122]

At least one landlord of the period, John Hamilton, in the same area, emulated McKnight in his use of Irish.[123] In 1835, a Presbyterian printer in Monaghan, Nat Greacen, produced *The Spiritual Rose*—a compendium of prayers in Irish—for Catholics. Many of the Catholic clergy, however, by their over-defensive attitude to Bible reading in Irish, accelerated the decline of Irish among their flocks. O'Donovan reported from Ballyjamesduff:

> ... the teachers of the bible through the medium of the Irish language have created in the minds of the peasantry a hatred for everything written in that language, and ... the society who encourage them could not have adopted a more successful plan to induce them to learn English and hate their own language.[124]

An often bitter controversy over the same subject between 1842 and 1844 was a major factor in the decline of Irish in the Glens of Antrim.[125] O'Donovan was a caustic enough observer and records a conversation with an old priest in Aghaderg concerning some of his colleagues. One reply indicated that many of them shared that pathetic attitude:

I asked him could the priests in general speak the language; he said they could, but as they were all young dandies from Maynooth they would not wish to let anyone know they understood a word of it, though, says he with a sneer, they never probably heard a word of English from their grandmothers nor probably from anyone until they were 12 years of age.[126]

Whatever about the hostile attitude of the early 19th-century Catholic clerics and a long period without mention in the *Records of the General Synod*, the official Presbyterian approach was quite different. The 1833 Synod of Ulster "passed an overture requiring a knowledge of Irish from some of their students" and, two years later, a study of Irish was made "imperative on candidates for holy orders"[127], while, in 1841, the General Assembly issued for their teachers an introduction to the Irish language, "our sweet and memorable mother tongue". As the Tempo Historical Society of Fermanagh said in their submission to the Opsahl Commission in 1993 " ... in the 19th century the Presbyterian Church was the only Irish church in which it was compulsory to learn Irish before ordination".[128]

FOUR

Ulster Protestants

and the Restoration

Throughout the period covered in the last chapter, Irish was on the retreat along the east coast and educational forces were among those causing the language shift. The charity schools inaugurated by Bishop Moule in 1712, "on the proposal that the whole nation may in time be made both Protestant and English", though not as widespread in Ulster as elsewhere[1], were one such force. Another was the 1731 charter schools "for the instruction of the children of the Irish natives in the English tongue and in the fundamental principles of the true religion".[2] (The National School system from 1831 onwards was, of course, to prove the largest single educational force towards anglicisation and this effect has often been so recorded by Ó Casaide[3], for example, and by Coupland[4].)

By the end of the 18th century, the decline had evoked an interest in revival, and this took practical form in the radical Belfast of the 1790s. A resolution of the Belfast Reading Society (from which came the Linenhall Library) on 2nd March, 1793

encouraged the obtaining and purchase of books and manuscripts in the Irish language.[5] A Loughinisland man, Pádraig Ó
Loingsigh, was teaching Irish then at the Belfast Academy[6] and
one of his pupils was 'The Man from God Knows Where', Thomas
Russell, of the Belfast Library, on whose grave in Downpatrick
Protestant cemetery Mary Ann McCracken set the slab bearing
the simple inscription 'The Grave of Russell'.[7] Ó Loingsigh,
probably through William Neilson, was in Dundalk in 1800
transcribing Irish manuscripts for "Samuel Coulter, a member
of the Presbyterian congregation there who employed
Donnchadh Mag Oireachtaigh, probably a local scribe". Samuel
Bryson, Andrew's father, probably spent some time there also.
Andrew was from Holywood, reared in Belfast and was minister
to the Ballymascanlon community from 1786 to 1795. In
themselves they represent the overlap between survival and
revival.[8] There is no doubting the extent of the revival at that
period. As Ernest Blythe put it, "Bhí sliocht na bPlandóirí á
nGaelú go tiubh an uair úd".[9] Another important feature of
the late 18th-century revival was the formation of the Belfast
Harp Society in 1791 "to revive and perpetuate the Ancient
Music and Poetry of Ireland".[10] Bryson was asked to assist at the
initial meetings to help with difficulties with the Irish language.[11]

The response to the 1791 advertisement being so good,
various committees were set up in Belfast to expand the work
of the Harp Society. Membership included Robert Bradshaw,
Robert Simms, Hon. Miss de Courcey, Mrs. John Clarke, Miss
Grant, Miss Bristow and Mrs. Kennedy. Among the more
important figures in this revival was the Cushendall Protestant
(son of a Catholic father), Dr. James Mac Donnell; Edward
Bunting, the Armagh Protestant, who was the first great collector of Irish music; and, as might be expected, the Joy and
McCracken families in Belfast. The harpers who assembled in
1792 were Art Ó Néill of Tyrone, Charles Fanning of Cavan,
Daniel Black and Denis Hempson from Derry, Charles Byrne
of Leitrim, Hugh Higgins of Mayo, Patrick Quinn and William

Carr from Armagh, Rose Mooney from Meath, and James Duncan from County Down.[12]

Mac Donnell (1762-1845) was separated by three generations from Sir Alastair Mac Colla Kittagh who had fought at Montrose's side, was kinsman to the earls of Antrim, and, with his brothers Randal and Alexander, was taught the harp by Art Ó Néill.

Hempson (O'Hamsey) was born in Derry in 1695, had known Carolan and played 'The King Shall Enjoy His Own Again' for Bonnie Prince Charlie in Edinburgh in 1745. He was regarded by Mac Donnell's friend Bunting as the last living exponent of the classical style of Irish harp-playing.

The blind Ó Néill had been an intimate of Echlin Ó Catháin and among his patrons were Charles O'Conor of Belnagare, Toby Peyton of Lisduff, Mrs. Crofton of Longford, Con O'Donnell of Larkfield and Squire Jones of Moneyglass.[13]

An interesting notice of Irish classes of the period reads:[14]

Irish Language

An attempt to revive the grammatical and critical knowledge of the Irish language in this town is generously made by Mr. Lynch: he teaches publicly in the Academy and privately in several families ... It is particularly interesting to all who wish for the improvement and Union of this neglected and divided kingdom. By our understanding and speaking it we could more easily and effectually communicate our sentiments and instructions to our Countrymen; and thus mutually improve and conciliate each other's affections.

The merchant and artist would reap great benefit from the knowledge of it. They would then be qualified for carrying on Trade and Manufactures in every part of their native country.

Later in the same year the *Northern Star* published the first ever Irish language magazine, *Bolg an Tsolair,* an 120-page miscellany of dialogue, poetry, translations, prayers and vocabulary. Lynch and Russell seem to have been its main begetters.[15] The purpose of *Bolg an Tsolair* was, as stated in the preface, "To recommend the Irish language to notice of Irishmen". That being so:

> ... any arguments laid down on that head, to persuade the natives that their own language is of some importance to them, would appear quite superfluous in the eyes of foreigners; but seeing that the Gaelic has been not only banished from the court, the college and the bar, but that many tongues and pens have been employed to cry it down and to persuade the ignorant that it was a harsh and barbarous jargon, and that their ancestors, from whom they derived it were an ignorant, uncultivated people—it becomes necessary to say something in reply ...
>
> The Irish enjoyed their own laws and language, till the reigns of Elizabeth and James, when English laws were universally established and English schools were erected with strict injunction that the vernacular tongue should be no longer spoken in the seminaries; yet ... even to this day the Irish is spoken by a great majority of the inhabitants of this kingdom ...
>
> It is chiefly with a view to prevent in some measure the total neglect, and to diffuse the beauties of this ancient and once-admired language that the following compilation is offered to the public, hoping to afford a pleasing retrospect to every Irishman, who respects the traditions, or considers the language and compositions of our early ancestors, as a matter of curiosity or importance.

The poetry in *Bolg an Tsolair* was collected and translated by Charlotte Brooke (who belonged to a cadet branch of the family now mostly represented in the public mind by Lord Brookeborough). Concerning her earlier work, the first anthology of Irish poetry to be printed, R.A. Breatnach has written:

> The honour of being the first literary critic, however, belongs not to Walker but to a remarkable lady named Charlotte Brooke, who in 1789 brought out a quarto volume of Ossianic poems and contemporary amhráin entitled *Reliques of Irish Poetry*. In many ways this is the most charming work on modern Irish Poetry known to me.[16]

In 1797 Bunting produced his first volume from his head-quarters—the McCracken household in Rosemary Lane, off High Street, where "in the bosom of rationalist Presbyterian Belfast the Renaissance of Irish music took place, the precursor by a century of the Irish Gaelic revival".[17]

If the United Irishman risings of 1798 and 1803 cost the revival movement many of its friends and leaders in dispersal, death or emigration (one thinks of Russell, McCracken, Tandy[18], Drennan and MacNevin—both Irish speakers, Lord Edward Fitzgerald, Wolfe Tone[19], Robert Emmet, William Putnam McCabe and Jemmy Hope[20]), the work went on in the north. Lynch, who with Mac Donnell was on the other side in the capture of their one time friend and colleague, Russell, was working on translations for Whitley Stokes at the end of the century and, in 1800, copying Irish manuscripts for Samuel Coulter (a supporter of the United Irishmen[21]) in Dundalk. Stokes published the gospels, *Na Ceithre Soisgeala*, in 1806 and followed this up with *Seanráite Sholaimh* in 1813.[22] It must not be thought that this was revivalism only—that was to come perhaps a century later, at a time when, through the growth of the city, there were about 8,000 Irish speakers in Belfast.[23]

Before looking at the subsequent Belfast scene in some detail, mention might be made of O'Donovan's compliment to Lord Farnham on spelling the names of townlands "very correctly", which seems to mark a knowledge of Irish[24]; of his observation that Fermanagh Irish approaches that of Connaught[25]; and of the story of Maxwell of Canningstown, who lost his inn in a court case about 1825 "because his records when produced in court were in Irish"![26]

FIVE

Restoration Belfast

The activities of the Belfast (*recte* Irish) Harp Society included
Irish classes. However haphazardly, such societies were aiming
at restoration of Irish—see for example this statement by the
Gaelic Society in Dublin:

> The Gaelic Society having for one of their foremost objects, the
> Revival of the language and literature of the Gaels ...[1]

It was this group which published Theophilus O'Flanagan's
edition of an Irish manuscript which the Countess of Moira
had bought and given to O'Flanagan, who acknowledged his
indebtedness to her.[2] Subscription lists can often indicate the
range of support for a publication. William Neilson's *Introduction to the Irish Language* was published by subscription in 1808
and among the subscribers were the Rev. Charles Akinson of
Forkhill, the Lord Bishop of Sodor and Man (William Ward
from Saintfield, County Down), Rev. Dr. Beaufort of Collon,

Alan Bellingham of Castlebellingham, S. Bryson of Belfast, Rev. W. S. Dickson in Keady, Sir Andrew Ferguson in Derry, George Gray at Graymount, Rev. Jas. Knox in Derry, T. Lloyd of Ravensdale, William Loftie in Tanderagee, Rev. Mr. McGin in Monagh, Rev. Mr. McDonogh in Cregan, Dr. Mac Donnell in Belfast, J. E. Ogle at Forkhill and G. Ogle of Newry, Joseph Pollock also at Newry, Sir John Sinclair, Thomas and John Stott of Dromore, S. H. Sloan in Markethill, Rev. R. Trail in Ballintoy and James Willis of Loughgall.

Neilson's *Grammar* was in use at the foot of Sliabh na nBan in Tipperary in the first quarter of the 19th century by the strong farmer, scribe, poet and revivalist Pádraig Ó Néill, who also used the first book ever published in the language, Seon Carsuel's *Foirm na nUrrnuidheadh* (The Book of Common Prayer) from 1567.[3]

One of the Irish classes held under the auspices of the Belfast Harp Society in No. 8 Pottinger's Entry on 17th July 1809, was attended by Rev. E. Groves, R. J. Tennant J. Riddel, William McClurkin, A. Mitchell, H. McDowell, A. McDowell and John MacAdam.[4] (The story of the organised groups in the Irish language movement in Belfast up to about 1860 has been told by Breandán Ó Buachalla in his 319-page study *I mBéal Feirste Cois Cuain* and much of the rest of the present section relies in large measure on his pioneering work.)

Dr. James Mac Donnell, one of the founders of the Belfast Harp Society, (under the auspices of which Art O'Neill taught seven or eight blind pupils until the society collapsed in 1813 when the doctor settled an annuity of £30 on O'Neill to keep him free from poverty) also founded the Belfast Dispensary (Belfast Charitable Institution) in 1792 and the Belfast Fever Hospital five years later. In turn, it was replaced in 1815 with a larger building in Frederick Street with an Irish manuscript in the centre of the foundation stone.[5] In 1801, he founded a precursor of the Gaelic League, the Literary Society, with Simms, Templeton, Henry Joy and Drennan. In 1810 the same element founded the Belfast Academical Institution (out of which Queen's University, Belfast, was to be formed eventually) and where Irish was taught by William Neilson from 1818 until 1821 and by Thomas Feenaghty from 1833 until 1849[6] and they partook in many other organisations—the Natural History and Philosophical Society, for example, and the Irish Harp Society which Mac Donnell and Bunting founded in 1808.[7] This society:

> ... was established primarily to provide blind boys and girls with the means of earning a living by teaching them the harp; secondarily to promote the study of the Irish language, history and antiquities.[8]

Its president was the Earl O'Neill. Other members included Bryson and Mac Donnell, both doctors, and Groves, a minister in the Church of Ireland, who was in charge of their Irish school. Another member was John McCracken, brother of Henry Joy, while yet another, John McGucken, had—to put it mildly—a very different background indeed.[9]

Among the most important people in the 19th-century movement were Samuel Bryson, son of the Rev. James Bryson mentioned earlier, and the MacAdam family. Bryson, from his early 20s had been a collector and copyist of old Irish manuscripts; his brother Andrew, a minister in Dundalk, was also an Irish speaker, and Samuel was a subscriber to Owen Connellan's *The Gospel According to St. John* in Irish (1830).[10]

Dr. William Neilson was accustomed to preach in Irish in Belfast and became professor of Hebrew and Oriental languages at the Academical Institution in 1819. While there, from 1818 until 1821, he established an Irish class, the prospectus for which said: "A Knowledge of the Modern Irish is, also, indispensable in travelling through many parts of Ireland where this language is still spoken".[11] (About 1860, the Rev. Mr. Steele preached in Irish to his Presbyterian congregation in Ballybofey on alternate Sundays.[12])

The Harp Society had found it difficult to continue due to lack of funds and in 1819 Neilson, with Joy, McCracken,

Templeton, Bristow, Orr, Tennant and Mac Donnell, began its
revival under the patronage of the Marquis of Hastings, the
Marquis of Downshire, Sir Francis McNaughton and Major
Charles Kennedy; and with over £1,000 collected by a supporting committee in Calcutta, among whom was Lt. Col. Casement
C.B., kinsman of Sir Roger Casement. In his time, Sir Roger,
who did so much for the cause of humanity in his reports from
the Congo and Putamayo, subscribed generously to Irish
colleges north and south, and wrote in the *Ulster Guardian* on
the 14th May 1913 that:

> When Irish history ceases to be written by buffoons and English
> music-hall artistes we shall begin to see that the simple title "an
> Irishman" is the common and glorious heritage of every son of the
> soil.[13]

The revived society lasted another 20 years, but by then a
more clearly *language*-orientated society was at work.[14] This was
Cuideacht Gaoidheilge Uladh [the Ulster Gaelic Society], founded
in 1830. Its driving forces were Dr. Mac Donnell, Dr. Reuben
J. Bryce and Robert S. MacAdam (a nephew of the Robert who
was governor of the Linenhall Library and who left a collection
of poems in Irish which he had gathered himself). Robert S.
MacAdam in 1828 had sent Tomás Ó Fiannachtaigh to
Ballynascreen to open an Irish school there.[15]

In 1828, Christopher Anderson's *Historical Sketches of the
Ancient Native Irish* was published. Having traced the history
and outlined the obtaining state of the Irish language, the
author argued trenchantly against the Government policy of
anglicisation, quoted the quondam bishop of Calcutta Reginald
Heber's assertion that the Government "was bent on a narrow
and illiberal policy of supplanting the Irish by the English
language"[16], demonstrated the wrong being done by keeping
people illiterate in their own language, and in one chapter
advocated "education through the medium of the Irish language, whether by means of Stationary or Circulating Schools".
He also stated that a Scottish Gaelic-speaking minister visiting

Ireland in 1827 had a congregation of 2,000.[17]

His recommendations were not accepted by the establishment of the day, whose 1831 National Education Act was probably the most important single factor in accelerating the decline of the Irish language.[18] In the short term, however, Anderson, who had been one of the most persistent agitators for the distribution of the Bible in Irish and for the education of the people to literacy in Irish and whose book was re-printed in 1830, had a considerable impact on the Marquis of Downshire. The Marquis wrote to Dr. Mac Donnell concerning Anderson's book:

> I have not yet read the book through but I have been led to think from the portion which I have perused that 'The Ancient Irish Literature' ought no longer to remain in the obscurity in which it has laid ...

Dr. Mac Donnell replied that what Anderson advocated was what their small society "have been wishing for and attempting" and he made the interesting observation about the book, that it:

> ... is written with great prudence and circumspection, for altho' the author be a Scotch Presbyterian yet one can never discern from this work to what sect he belongs. There is none of those absurd reproaches cast upon the Papist, no predictions of their conversion, nothing said about Antichrist, the Babylonesh Lady and the beast with ten horns.

Downshire, whose father had been a patron of the Harp Society and whose brother was fluent in Irish—as were his children and agents—and a collector of Irish manuscripts, became president of Cuideacht Gaoidheilge Uladh, Mac Donnell being the chairman, with MacAdam and Bryce as secretaries.[19]

The Society and its members, mostly-middle class Belfast Presbyterians, were not only teaching and organising Irish

classes, lobbying, corresponding with similarly disposed people (for example, Phillip Barron of Waterford), and publishing
in Irish. They were also extremely active in collecting, copying
and editing old Irish manuscripts and in commissioning scribes
around the country to record as many recent compositions as
had only been in oral circulation beforehand (all of which was
a major contribution to scholarship and to creativity). MacAdam
purchased a large collection in Dublin in 1830 and copied and
translated a long account of the O'Neill wars of 1641-47 from
a manuscript then in the possession of Earl O'Neill (who,
incidentally, was also a patron of the Iberno-Celtic Society
founded in 1818).[20]

Their first publication was a translation by Thomas Finnerty
(Feenaghty) of Maria Edgeworth's *Forgive and Forget (Maith
agus Dearmad)* and *Rosanna* in 1833. Dr. Bryce knew Maria
Edgeworth and presumably it was he who obtained her permis-
sion to have the translation made and published. Bryce and
MacAdam signed the dedication of the book to Downshire.[21]

The teaching of Irish had lapsed at the Academical Institution but the decision of the Synod of Ulster "making the study
of Irish imperative on their candidates for holy orders" made
the professorship of Irish at the Institute imperative also. In
1833, it was given to Tomás Ó Fiannachtaigh, who realised that
"In the article of class books, a great want exists" and that "The
chief obstacle of the reviving the cultivation of the Irish
language is the want of elementary books". To remedy part of
this MacAdam and he published their grammar, *An Introduction to the Irish Language intended for the use of Irish Classes in the
Royal Belfast Academical Institution* in 1835. This had been
printed in Dublin: MacAdam, in letters to Barron in Waterford, was hoping to move Barron's press to Belfast for succeeding
publications.[22]

Though founding the Soho Foundry in Townsend Street by
Robert and James MacAdam in 1835 took up much of their
time, Robert remained involved in the teaching of Irish, in the
collection of manuscripts, in publication and in setting up of

schools. In 1837, they published *Bolg a Tsolair: An Céud Roinn* by Finnerty also, apparently, printed in Belfast this time, as the first of a projected series aimed at schools. (Anderson published his translation of the first half of Bunyan's *Pilgrim's Progress* the same year.) The motto of *Bolg an Tsolair* was:

Is tír gan tlacht, gan reacht, gan fhéile
Nach d-tuigeann treabh aon Máthar a chéile.

In 1838, their next title—a grammar with conversation pieces and spiritual reading—was published: *An Irish Primer Compiled and Published Under the Patronage of the Ladies Gaelic Society* (apparently an offshoot of the Cuideacht, as was the Drogheda Gaelic Society). Two years later, Bunting's third volume of *Ancient Music of Ireland* appeared.[23]

An interesting by-product of the Belfast Irish classes was the interest of past pupils in translations from Irish. Among them were Samuel Ferguson, Thomas O'Hagan, and George Fox. Matthew Graham published *The Giantess from the Irish of Oisin*, Belfastman Henry Riddell Montgomery (who was an advocate of the teaching of Irish) published his *Early Native Poetry* in 1846 and the Rev. William Hamilton Drummond of Larne produced his translations of *Ancient Irish Minstrelsy* in 1852.[24]

In 1841, George Field, sometime agent for the Home Mission, a correspondent of MacAdam's and then apparently living in Scotland, had his grammar published in Belfast. Its title was *Casán na Gaedhilge, An Introduction to the Irish language; compiled at the request of the Irish Teachers; under the patronage of the General Assembly in Ireland, And Dedicated to them as a tribute of esteem for their zeal in preserving and extending the knowledge of our beloved Mother tongue, By their friend and countryman, S.O.M. (Seorsa Ó Mhachaire).* Field, whom Ó Baoill (*op. cit.*, p.166) mistakenly assumes used the name 'Ó Domhnaill' as a pseudonym (Hugh McDonnell/Aodh Ó Domhnaill wrote the items referred to) also, according to Ó Baoill, had a poem dedicated to him by Cathal Ó Carbhólan around 1840, and also translated "the

Westminster Shorter Catechism with Scripture proofs, into the Irish language". No copy of this is known to have survived, if published.

In the preface to the *Casán* Field wrote:

> This work has been compiled for the use of the Native Irish and for those who wish to acquire a knowledge of our sweet and venerable mother tongue. Its chief aim is to remove some of the obstacles which usually present themselves to both and thus to promote the study of a language, which, like the ivy, conceals while it preserves beneath its graceful leaves, the 'mingled beauties' of intellect and art. To this end the grammars of O'Brien, O'Reilly, Neilson, Halliday, Connellan and Feenachty and also those of Stewart and Munroe, have rendered valuable service. I have likewise to acknowledge the assistance and instruction afforded by Michael McNulty, Hugh McDonnell, Michael Branagan and other native Irishmen.

(These were teachers or officials of the Irish Society: McNulty teaching in Leitrim, Gordon in Co. Down and later in Kerry, while Branagan was on the committee in 1827. They were later in agreement with the Irish Society, working under the auspices of the Home Mission set up by the Synod of Ulster in 1836.) When, as a result of pressure against the Home Mission in the Glens, Hugh McDonnell was, in effect, forced out of employment, MacAdam hired him and brought him in Belfast as his assistant in tracing, copying, compiling and annotating Irish manuscripts.[25]

McDonnell was one of the Oriel school of poets and an important scribe for MacAdam. Poet, historian, teacher and scribe, his was a sad enough life, though fruitful. Among the Catholic teachers employed with McDonell in the Bible schools was Art Mac Bionaid who satirized Dr. Butler, the one-time Catholic priest in Newry who had changed his religion[26], and often disparaged McDonnell himself.[27] Another who could be mentioned was James Wood, Séamus Mac Giolla Choille, Doctor and chemist in Dundalk who:

... held the last Iomarbhá, or Bardic Contention, we have known to
be held in Ireland 1825 and 1826

and was married to Anne Tyrrell who died 1859 and was buried
in the Protestant Churchyard in Dundalk.[28] Art Mac Cumhaigh
(Art McCooey) also wrote of the contention between the
'Róimhchill' and the 'Teampall Gallda'. He himself was married in a Protestant church![29]

McDonnell left Belfast in 1856, returning to his old job of
Bible-teaching again, this time in Donegal, probably facilitated
in this by Cathal Ó Cearbhalláin who had been a Catholic but
became a Protestant and who wrote the poem about George
Field already mentioned. Ó Cearbhalláin was married to
McDonnell's daughter, Anna.[30]

MacAdam had agents and correspondents from Meath to
Donegal and was succeeding so well that, in 1844, he wrote: "I
think I perceive the dawn of a better day for Irish Literature"[31].
As McDonnell wrote of him then:

Is fear fearúil an Mac Ádaimh sin a thug grá mór don Ghaeilge,
A bhíos cumannach dáimhiúil le bard agus éigse.

Certainly not only was he saving and recording a tremendous amount from oral tradition, but he had provoked,
encouraged or inspired a considerable number of new compositions, some of which Ó Buachalla has published[32], and one of
which—Hugh McDonnell's elegy on the death of Dr. James
Mac Donnell *Tuireadh an Dochtúir Mhic Dhomhnaill*—MacAdam
had printed in Belfast in 1845.[33]

One sad echo of the Bible controversy in the Glens was that
the efforts of their last Gaelic poet, an ancestor of Major James
Chichester-Clarke, could not stay the decline of the language
there.[34] However, if Clare, also a comparatively recently lost
Gaeltacht, can boast its Protestant poet Micheál Coimín
(Comyn)[35], the Protestant poet from the Glens, uncle of Sir
Daniel Dixon and a man well-known to Eoin Mac Neill's

mother, John McCambridge transmitted to us one of the best loved songs in Irish, the haunting 'Aird a' Chumhaing'.[36]

SIX

Decline and Survival

While MacAdam continued and remained at work on his 1388-page English-Irish Dictionary, compiled out of 'Méad mo ghean ar mo thír dhúchais agus ... teasghrá don teangaidh' (the manuscript of which is now in the Queen's University, Belfast), political developments and the rapid growth of Belfast added to all the factors listed by Ó Casaide[1] and to more besides, meant that the great years of the Cuideacht and its work were past. This was apparent in some ways and not so apparent in others. The Cuideacht seems to have ceased effective functioning about 1843 and, with the foundation of Queen's College, Belfast, the Academical Institution gave up its Irish classes[2], though Irish was still taught under Bryce at the Academy into the 1880s. Queen's did have a chair in Irish, to which O'Donovan was appointed in 1849, the year of Queen Victoria's visit to Belfast where she was greeted by a large banner with its legend in Irish.[3]

Ó Néill spoke of the decline in this period, attributing it "to two causes, first the utter failure of '98 which brought in its train a disillusionment with revolutionary ideas, and ultimately a rejection even of liberalism; secondly to the pressure of industrialisation which changed Belfast from the pleasant enlightened town it had been into a mass of dark Satanic mills, where there was little room for culture of any kind". Mac Adam thought the decline was caused by "scholars who had no interest in the living language; writers using obscure language; the attitude of the Catholic Church, neglecting to teach Catechism and to give sermons in the language ... and the efforts of the Protestant Church to beguile the poor Catholics from their faith, the only result being that it had done more harm to the language than foreign persecution for 300 years".[4]

But as an indication of the decline in public interest, of hostility, or of both, Irish was not a normal B.A. subject in Queens. O'Donovan, accordingly, had very few pupils and spent most of his time in Dublin except for the annual series of public lectures which he gave and with the success of which he expressed satisfaction.[5] On his death in 1862, the post was not filled, despite repeated representation. Samuel Ferguson, who insisted on competence in Irish being an essential qualification for anyone working in the Public Record Office, reported on one such effort in 1875:

> We have done our endeavour to found such a chair here, but all things Celtic are regarded by our educated classes as of questionable *ton* and an idea exists that it is not expedient to encourage anything tending to foster Irish sentiment.

Irish was not taught again in Queen's until 1909 and the professorship not re-established until 1945.[6]

Mac Adam, however, was working away, as were some of his scribes[7], but Ó Buachalla cannot trace any manuscripts written in Irish in Belfast after 1854.[8]

To an extent the focus, in terms of revivalism, turns on Dublin at this stage. Isaac Butt, from Donegal, and Rev. E.G. Hudson, Dean of Armagh, were vice-presidents of the Celtic

Society, which held its first annual meeting early in 1848.[9] John Mitchel (born in 1815), whose father—a dissenting minister— had played a small part in 1798[10], was probably an Irish speaker[11], and he had been on the council of the Celtic Society before his deportation to Van Diemen's Land.[12]

Mitchel, writing about the famine in the *Nation* in 1847, spoke of the cottages where "our ears drank in the honey-sweet tones of the well-beloved Gaelic" and asked rhetorically:

> But why do we not see the smoke curling from these lowly chimneys ... Oh, misery! had we forgotten that this was the *Famine Year*. Ah! they are dead! they are dead! the strong man and the fair dark eyed woman and the little ones with their liquid Gaelic accents that melted into music for us two years ago.

No doubt he had hit on one of the major causes of the language decline.

His friend, comrade, fellow Ulsterman and brother-in-law, John Martin, complained of the delay in publishing an Irish dictionary—he had put up (the then enormous sum of) £200 for the project two years earlier.[13] This may well have been MacAdam's Dictionary which was supposed to be ready for printing in 1850.[14]

In 1852 MacAdam was in charge of the Irish history and antiquities section of the major exhibition mounted in Belfast on the occasion of the twenty second meeting of the British Association for the Advancement of Science. He exhibited many of his Irish manuscripts at this and the exhibition succeeded so well that, in 1853, he launched the *Ulster Journal of Archeology*, which he continued to edit and finance until 1862. In its first edition, he wrote of the debt the Irish language and history owed to Ussher, Ware, Nicholson, Hutchenson and Vallencey, "nor must we omit that of our townsman, Dr. Neilson, to whose exertions, at a critical moment, we are, perhaps, indebted for a renewed interest in the ancient language of Ireland". He seemed somewhat depressed about the state of the language, writing in the same preface that:

> We are on the eve of great changes. Society in Ulster seems breaking up. Old things and old notions are passing away so rapidly, that the events appear to be but shifting scenes in the drama of a night ... That which conquest and colonization failed to effect in centuries, steam and education, are now accomplishing peacefully and rapidly.[15]

While the times were a-changing, Adam published one more work of perennial significance—the 500 proverbs he had collected all over the northern half of Ireland. Published by him in the *UJA* they form the basis of Enrí Ó Muirgheasa's *Seanfhocla Uladh* published initially in 1907.[16]

That change could be demonstrated by a middle-class Protestant example. Up to about 1850 it was every bit as normal for a member of that class in society to be a member of the Harp Society or of Cuideacht Gaoidheilge Uladh as it was to belong to the Literary Society or to the Natural History and Philosophical Society. After, say, 1860, such being the by-products of political tension, the Irish language began to become more and more associated in the public mind with Catholicism (despite the continued existence of communities of Irish-speaking Protestants, such as those on Rathlin Island, what was left at Ballymascanlon and in parts of Donegal, and despite the controversy 20 years earlier in the Glens when it was the Presbyterians who were on the side of Irish, whereas the reaction of the Catholic clergy "destroyed along the Antrim coast the Irish language", in the words of the Rev. Monsignor James O'Laverty).[17] While Irish continued to be spoken in the north, it was looked on with a certain suspicion by the people who had no firsthand knowledge of it, and who seldom met Irish speakers (many of whom had little or no literacy in it).[18]

While some of this survival could be described as sparks from raked embers—for example, the Irish words in the scrap books of James Breakey of Drumskelt at the end of century[19], it could still produce Irish speakers of the calibre of Dr. James MacKnight from Rathfriland (1801-1876), sometime editor of the *Belfast Newsletter* and the *Derry Standard*, quondam Tenant Leaguer and Land Reformer[20]. It still could produce Irish-speaking scholars of the order of the Rev. Robert King—longtime headmaster of Ballymena Academy, author of a number of books in Irish who lived until the turn of the century[21], and Dr. William Reeves (1815-1892), bishop of Down, Connor and Dromore, historian and pioneer in the study of east Ulster placenames.[22]

Mac Adam had been responsible for the inclusion of those sections, which supplied data towards an assessment of the extent of the Irish-speaking population, in the 1851 census.[23] While he did not expect the returns to be accurate:

> It is well known that in various districts where the two languages co-exist, but where English now predominates, numbers of individuals returned themselves as ignorant of the Irish language either from a false sense of shame or from a secret dream that the Government in making this enquiry (for the first time) had some concealed motive, which could not be for their good ...

This is a view with which O'Donovan concurred. The census returns—for all their shortcomings—still constitute a most useful tool for the investigator of the pattern of language shift.[24] Another difficulty with the census is that the barony was the smallest unit for which separate language statistics were given.[25] According to the statistics Irish was the prevailing language in Donegal. There were more than 10,000 Irish speakers in each of the counties Armagh, Monaghan, Cavan, and Tyrone. Most of the 5,000 Irish speakers in Co. Derry were in the Barony of Loughinsholin, while most of Antrim's 3,000 were in Lower Glenarm and Cary. Down had the least number, though there was an Irish-speaking community in Upper Iveagh. Overall the Irish-speaking population in Ulster was 6.8 per cent.[26] In 1911—the last occasion before 1991 in which the number of Irish speakers was recorded in a census covering what is now Northern Ireland—the percentage there had fallen to 2.3 per cent of the population.[27]

If, in terms of the Anglo-Irish dialectology, the areas of

Northern or Ulster speech (which "includes part of Leitrim, Cavan and North Meath" with "a southeastern salient" stopping "not so very far northwest of Dublin"[28]) approximates, except for its southwestern segment, to the Old Irish North-South divide of Leth Cuinn and Leth Moga[29], the returns of the 1851 census mark what is, perhaps, a more significant divide—an East-West one: 6.8 per cent spoke Irish in Ulster in 1851, 4.3 per cent spoke it in Leinster (whereas in Connacht and Munster the percentages were 51 per cent and 44 per cent respectively).[30] If there was no significant Irish-speaking community in County Down, for example, in 1891, neither was there any in Wicklow, Wexford, Carlow, Westmeath, Laois or Offaly.

In his speech in Kilkenny, on 25th February 1993, Chris McGimpsey referred to the pleas of the (still) anonymous Belfast author of the letter referred to by Cathal O'Byrne in *As I Roved Out—A Book of the North* (Dublin, 1946, pp.173, 174). The author, addressing "true hearted Irishmen and Irishwomen", says:

> To one possessing the English language, the study of Irish affords the greatest educational advantage, the two languages being as different ... as two sister tongues in the Indo-European family ... can be.
>
> No other country in Europe supplies records exhibiting phases of thought and civilisation so archaic as are afforded by the Irish Annals. The period from which the Irish Historical Annals start is so remote that in other countries nothing has been preserved to compare with it. It is estimated that close upon one thousand MSS. in our libraries lie untranslated and unpublished.
>
> Are we to allow that still-living language in which these venerable records are preserved to become dead? Are we to become aliens in speech and thought to all the greatest characters in our history? If we so act, we are unworthy of the rich heritage which has been bequeathed to us, incomparable in its value.
>
> To anyone having a knowledge of Irish the names in daily use of our townlands and other localities no longer appear as meaningless counters without superscription—they at once start into life,

and the legend on the currency furnishes a word-picture that paints the characteristic feature of the scene; recalls some deed of daring, some curious tradition or the memory of some great piety. Every hill, every stream and valley in the land calls upon us to preserve our ancient tongue. If we neglect it, and it is allowed to die, we suffer a loss that is irreparable—our living connection with an ancient and honoured past will be severed. A great floating literature will be forever lost—hymns, ballads, poems, proverbs, folklore and historic tradition—such as no other nation possess.

A Spaniard speaks Spanish; a Russian, Russian; a Greek, Greek; an Italian, Italian; a Frenchman, French; a German, German; an Englishman, English; an Irishman—Is this an honourable thing? Are we content to allow our children to receive an education which leaves them ignorant of the Irish language? To our credit or discredit is the answer.

MacAdam died early in 1895 and the first branch of the Gaelic League (Conradh na Gaeilge) was founded in Belfast later that year.[31]

SEVEN

Ulster Protestants
and the Gaelic League

The foundation of Conradh na Gaeilge by a Glens Catholic and a Connacht Protestant in Dublin in 1893 was the first really major move towards rediffusion. Cathal O'Byrne could write that:

> With the advent of the Gaelic League the language came, at least partly, into its own. But the League was never considered quite 'respectable'—that awful Belfast word—by planters. To be a Gaelic Leaguer was to be suspect always ...[1]

But, nonetheless, Protestants were members from the beginning in Belfast, something which still obtains. Some may have come into it from earlier organisations; we know that the League's first vice-president, the Rev. Euseby Digby Cleaver, had been vice-president of the Ossianic Society long years before that.[2] The first president of the League in Belfast was the Hollywood Presbyterian Dr. St. Clair Boyd who spoke of the

tragedy of the decline of "such a beautiful and noble language"[3] (a contrast with some English newspaper insults early
in the century—the *Morning Post* called Irish 'Kitchen Kaffir'
and the *Daily Mail* described it as "a barbarous language").[4]

The Belfast Branch's initial meeting took place in the
Catholic Donegalman P.T. McGinley's house, 32 Beersbridge
Road. He was later, and often, the president—nationally—of
the entire League. The first Belfast branch grew naturally out
of the Irish language classes initiated in the Belfast Naturalists'
Field Club (of which MacAdam had been at the helm for so
long) in 1892. St. Clair Boyd was a member of that club also and
F.J. Bigger began attending Irish classes there in 1894.

Activities in the branch, which soon stood at 120 members
included visits to the Gaeltacht areas still surviving in the Glens,
Omeath and Draperstown; St. Clair Boyd in his first Annual
General Meeting address referring to their surprise at the
"extent of spoken Irish in east Ulster".

The first play written in Irish was by McGinley and it was first
performed in Belfast in 1900.

They issued a statement in 1897 condemning a Resident
Magistrate, William Orr, who had sentenced a man in
Dungarvan for giving evidence in Irish.

Almost in reverse of the revival of 100 years earlier, when the
language followed the music so to speak, the first Feis Cheoil
was held in Dublin in 1897, Belfast hosting the second in 1898.
The patrons there were Lady Annesley of Castlewellan and
Lady Arthur Hill of Gilford. On its committee were Charles H.
Brett, John St. Clair Boyd, F. J. Bigger, W.G. Churchill, M.
Crymble, W.H. Derrick-Large, the Lord Mayor James
Henderson and Robert Young.[5]

The League's 1897-8 session in Belfast included an address
by Alexander Graham of Inverness, who surprised his audi-
ence with the ease with which he could be understood.[6] Irish
classes were organised in the Museum under the auspices of
the Belfast Naturalists' Field Club.[7] On 10th November 1897,
they presented an address to one of their patrons, Canon

Crozier of the Church of Ireland, on the occasion of his transfer to Kilkenny. They printed his reply, in which he said:

> As foghlaim na Gaeilge le chéile agus as a meas coiteann ar an teanga is amhlaigh a thiocfaidh méadú ar mheas na ndaoine dá chéile a raibh grá na tíre á spreagadh ar aon[8] [From learning the language together and from their general regard for it, mutual respect will grow among people whose love of country inspired them all.]

These sentiments echothose of O'Donovan's friend, Dr. William Reeves.[9]

The prominent Orangeman Dr. R.R. Kane, who was an Irish-speaker and who is said to have signed the minutes of the Lodge of which he was the Master in Irish[10], supported the Gaelic League at its inception, as did Charles Percy Bushe and J.H. Lloyd.[11] Canon J.O. Hannay ('George Birmingham') was on the national executive of the Conradh in 1906[12], and Lindsay Crawford, founder of the Independent Orange Order, is listed as a candidate for the executive in 1907[13] and as opening Nenagh Feis in 1909.[14]

The League grew in Belfast. There were nine branches in 1899 and in one public meeting, Logue, in the chair, said the language was "affording a common platform to Catholic and Protestant, Gael, Sean-Ghall and Nua-Ghall, north and south". A Belfast regional executive (Coiste Ceantair) was formed, a Belfast College of Irish with Bigger as its patron in 1905 (it lasted until 1923) as was a provincial assembly for Ulster, Dáil Uladh the same year. This Dáil ran the Ulster Irish Training College in the Donegal Gaeltacht.[15]

It was probably as a result of Gaelic League activities that the percentage of Irish speakers in what is now Northern Ireland rose from 1.3 per cent in 1891 to 2.3 per cent in 1911 (and almost 10.7 in 1991)[16]. One example of this is the return of a comparatively large number of Irish speakers in Moneyrea which "may have been due to the efforts of the Rev. Richard Lyttle, the Unitarian minister in Co. Down of Moneyrea (ob.

1908) who was a keen Gaelic Leaguer and organised classes in his area to get people interested in Irish".[17] Because of this, too, the *Church of Ireland Gazette* in 1904 said "we are Irishmen, and ... we must be prepared to accept along with the honour conferred by the title the duties which it involves. One of those duties is the preservation of the Irish language".[18]

One of the many who went through the League then was the Quaker educationalist William Glynn (Liam Mag Fhloinn), 1895-1993, from Belfast, who taught for years at the Friends' School in Lisburn. He said, "for us in Ireland Irish has a particular value. Through it we get ... to the ... underlying spirits of this centuries' old community which is 'Ireland' ... Irish has enabled me to become a freeman of Ireland".[19] Another was Lil Nic Dhonnchadha's father who died in 1918. Lil (born Lilian Duncan) in Belfast joined Cumann Gaelach na hEaglaise (the Irish Society within the Church of Ireland among whose patrons have been Dr. G.O. Simms and Dr. Donal Caird) at its inception in 1914. One of her teachers of Irish at T.C.D. was E. J. Gwynn, later provost. Later she was principal of Coláiste Móibhí, the training college for Protestant primary school teachers where her predecessor was another Ulster Protestant, Seán A. Ó Cadhla (John A. Kyle).

Lil published an Irish hymnal—including some of her own compositions—in 1961, co-operated with Simms and Canon Blenerhasset in services through Irish and with Cosslett Quin, the Rev. Sydney Craig and the Rev. Frank Hipwell in the 1965 edition of the Book of Common Prayer in Irish. Highly regarded, she was at one time President of the Oireachtas, the annual Irish cultural festival on the lines of the Scottish Mod or Welsh Eisteddfod.[20]

The Cumann Gaelach had the support of Casement among others, including Thomas O'Neill Russell, the Moate-born member of the Gaelic League predecessor, the Society for the Preservation of the Irish Language, and the Orangeman from Lisburn Dr. George St. George who signed a petition for services in Irish at St. Patrick's Cathedral in Dublin. (They did have such a funeral service for one of their members in Templepatrick at that time.[21])

In January 1906, Cumann Gaelach an Choláiste was founded in Queen's by the historian of 1798, Charles Dickson (a Unitarian); Frank Ferran, a medical doctor from Magherafelt, who later died a republican prisoner in the Curragh in 1922; J.H. Harbison; and W.P. MacArthur, "a Presbyterian who was educated in Bangor"; whose 'father', Dr. Dickson said, "had a little Irish", who "by his own efforts was a fully competent speaker" and who "became Lieutenant-General Sir William MacArthur Director General of the R.A.M.C".[22] The other members of the committee were "Miss Lynd, B.A.; Mr. J. L. Lynd, B.A.; Mr. James Ferguson, B.A".[23] They launched an agitation for the restoration of a lectureship in Irish in Queen's and they were successful when the Rev. Canon Feardorcha Ó Conaill—a native Irish speaker and a Rector's son—was appointed at £250 a year plus the curacy of St. George's. The Gaelic League offered to pay half of his salary for five years if the authorities would make him a full Professor. This was agreed to initially, but the decision was later reversed, something which led Ó Conaill, 'Conall Cearnach', to compose a long satire on the topic (in the metre of *Hiawatha*), which he later published in the *Ulster Guardian.*[24]

One of their earlier supporters was the Presbyterian classics professor R.M. Henry who died in 1950, well-loved and respected and the subject on his death of an affectionate farewell poetic homage from John Hewitt.

At an early meeting in 1908, they were addressed by Mac Arthur and P.T. McGinley, Mac Giolla Phádraig (Lord Castletown), Rev. J.O. Hannay ('George Birmingham'), Capt. Otway-Cuffe and McHenry.[25]

Ó Glaisne lists among Protestants in the early Gaelic League Seán O'Casey, Gough, Emily Gough (first cousin to Lord Gough), The Hon. Albinia Broderick (Gobnait Ní Bhruadair) and F.J. Bigger. In the 5 Provinces Branch in Dublin (nicknamed the branch of the 5 Protestants), there were many

Protestants, some obviously from Ulster. Among them he listed Lil Nic Dhonnchadha, Dora French, Margaret and Sadhbh Trench (Trinseach)—daughters of the Archbishop of Dublin, Nora Cunningham, Máire Scarlóid, three Williams sisters including the artist Lily. Others mentioned by him in other branches included James Stephens the writer, Robert Lynd, Sam Maguire, Aodh de Blácam, Stephen Gwynn, Edith Drury, Seamus Deacon (Deakin), who was in the Irish Republican Brotherhood, as was George Irvine.[26]

In Belfast, he lists Seán Lester, Seán Best, Herbert Moore Pim and Jimmy Snoddy (probably a kinsman of my own).[27]

Seán Mac Maoláin recalls collecting for the League early in the century in a large Belfast bakery where he was apprenticed and where most of the staff were Protestant and getting a half-sovereign from one of them who said:

> A subscription for the Irish language. Why wouldn't I? Sure, every country should have its own language. And maybe you don't know, but I heard plenty of Irish when I was a young man. I was working in a Newry Bakery at that time, and I had some good friends among the people that used to come in from Killeavey on market days. And I learned a good wheen of Irish words from one old fellow that I had many's a pint with. Listen! Do you know the meaning of this: Slanty go seel agad agus ban er du veen ugad?[28]

Other prominent Protestants in the Gaelic League in the early years of the century were Mrs. Arthur Hutton, who translated *An Táin*, Róis Ní Ógáin (daughter of Major Chichester Young and compiler of a three-volume anthology of Irish verse), and two who will always be associated with the Feis in the Glens—Ada MacNeill, kinswoman of Lord Cushendun, and Margaret Dobbs, who was secretary of the Feis at its inception in 1904—and for half a century afterwards.[29]

In letters in 1912 to Lady Constance Emmot in Argyle, Roger Casement wrote about the Gaeltacht in Scotland, his support for Irish-medium schools, the Donegal Gaeltacht, the Rathlin Irish Teaching Scheme he was involved in and the strengthening of the language about Cloughaneely in Donegal.[30]

Another north Antrim Protestant lady involved in matters Irish was Helen Macnaghten of Bushmills. Her extensive correspondence with Anne Richardson is redolent of the atmosphere of those days in the language movement in north Antrim. She talks of a Gaelic concert in the Ulster Hall (around 1895), a visit to the Irish College in Gortahork with two friends (around1910), an occasion in the Albert Hall (around 1910) "as exciting as a big Gaelic League meeting", the Irish in Rathlin, the Claremorris controversy with McHannay—J.O. Hannay, one presumes—(again no date but, probably, around 1910), the Oireachtas, Dineen's *Dictionary*, the growth of the Gaelic League, Lady Desart's article on the League in *The Nineteenth Century*, her project to start an Irish training college in Ulster.[31]

Prominent also were Bulmer Hobson, Alice Milligan and Robert Lynd (grand-uncle to Sir Robert Lowry) who wrote:

> The 'Real Irishman' is neither essentially a Celt nor essentially a Catholic. He is merely a man who has the good or bad fortune to be born in Ireland or of Irish parents, and who is interested in Ireland more than any other country in the world ... The Orange labourer of the north whose ancestors may have come from Scotland, has all the attributes of an Irishman no less than the Catholic labourer of the west, whose ancestors may have come from Greece, or from Germany, or from Spain, or from anywhere you care to speculate.[32]

In the summer of 1994, the first of a projected sequence of busloads of Irish learners from the Shankill went for a refresher course in the Donegal Gaeltacht[33], an echo of the fact that one of the League's first northern branches was on the Shankill[34], and that in the 1911 census 106 people recorded themselves as Irish speakers there as did 547 in Smithfield, 529 in Ormeau, 302 in Windsor and 98 in St. George's.[35]

EIGHT

Modern Attitudes
to the Language

The ignorance and apprehension, that John Magee wrote about[1] still obtain in some measure:

> For many Ulstermen Irish culture and Irish separatism had become synonymous terms. This explains their astonishing antipathy towards the Irish language—though it involved a rejection of a field of scholarship in which Ulster Protestants such as Charlotte Brooke, Bishop Reeves, Samuel Bryson, Robert MacAdam, Sir Samuel Ferguson and Margaret Dobbs are only some of the most prominent names. The consequences of this rejection for the young people in our schools were to my mind wholly regrettable. Celtic mythology, legends and heroic tales, Irish dancing and music—even *Moore's Melodies*—were jettisoned in an effort to show that Ulster children were different from the rest of Irishmen, a people apart. In many Protestant schools children grew up with no knowledge of the traditions of the country in which they lived and to which they were attached by every human feeling.

Yet there remains a comparatively untapped vein of good-will, as in this statement:

> The Presbyterian Church co-operated with the government of northern and southern Ireland in anything which will preserve the art, culture, and literature of the country and which will instil in people a pride in, and love for their land ...
>
> The Presbyterian Church in Ireland is a national church and knows no border in its work but seeks to serve God in all parts of the land ... because it is Irish it is proud of its native background[2]

It is also shown by the publication in 1970 of the New Testament translated into Irish by the Derriaghy born Church of Ireland Canon, Cosslett Ó Cuinn, President of Oireachtas na Gaeilge in 1972 and again in 1973.

In 1962, the editor of *An tUltach* asked a number of people their opinions about the preservation and restoration of Irish. Dr. James Scott expressed himself very much in favour of the teaching of Irish; Jack Loudan expressed regret at not having learned it in his youth and was in favour of the preservation of Irish culture; the Northern Ireland Labour Party chairman, Charles Brett, was against the revival but in favour of antiquarian study; Sir Charles Larmor, while having little against the revival of Irish, and realising its being part of his heritage, was dubious about the possibility of its revival; Richard Hayward was also dubious on this level but advocated strongly the teaching of Irish in schools, as did the Rev. P.H. Rogers of Portora; John Irvine regretted that he had not learned Irish, but, like Denis Ireland, was very much in favour of it: "Bheinn go mór i leith na Gaeilge a chur chun cinn." While B. Mac K. McGuigan was against the revival he was in favour of Irish being taught in schools, as was Sir Robert Cunningham.[3] Denis Ireland had been a member of the Gaelic Fellowship founded by the Presbyterian civil servant John Pasker (1903-1965) in the mid-40s within the YMCA:

> to provide a means whereby Protestants may contact others who

know or wish to learn Gaelic and in due course unite for Church services in Gaelic.[4]

It is, I suggest, ignorance of their history that led some Loyalist extremists to adopt an Enoch Powellite inversion of the Algerian situation and to suggest that non-Unionists are foreigners in Northern Ireland.[5] Jack Loudan once said that if he were Minister for Education he would give primacy to Irish history, placenames and folklore. Richard Hayward said that the outlook of many people ignorant of and disrespectful towards their heritage was bound to be shallow.[6] Brian Faulkner expressed hostility to Irish in 1973[7] as did Roy Bradford.[8] Bradford eased on his position later even using a few sentences in Irish in one article.[9] The Orange Order's journal in 1980 speaking of the 'Irish Language in Decline', did so with genuine concern and interest.[10] Kenneth Jamison, then Director of the Arts Council of Northern Ireland, made this plea in December 1969:

> Only in Ulster do we ourselves make the quite unnecessary equation between traditional culture and politics, and thus leave ourselves bereft of any tradition, of any real sense of identity ... I am convinced that a rediscovery rather than a continuing rejection of Ulster's traditional culture is something we should seek to achieve both for its own intrinsic worth and for the new sense of unity it gives to the Ulster people.[11]

It is the purpose of this study to show that the Irish language is an important stratum in that tradition and of that heritage. It has been obscured, through short-sighted educational policies, from the people of Northern Ireland. Most of their placenames, for example, are Irish, though hard to recognise as such and often impossible to understand the garbled phonetics of whichever English civil servant transcribed them from the Irish. Belfast, Coleraine, Shankill are all Irish words in disguise. Most of the music of the northern Protestant is of a common root and of a common heritage: indeed the

Englishman's skit on Tyrconnell and now an Orange ballad 'Lilliburlero' is macaronic—'Lilliburlero Bullenalaw' being corrupt transcripts of Irish phrases: *an Lile ba Léir Dhó, Ba Linn an Lá*, perhaps.[12]

Christopher McGimpsey[13] refers to the Irish inscription on the banner of the "ill-fated Ireland's Heritage LOL 1303"[14], (which has not been heard of publicly since the Kincora scandal involved its founder William McGrath). The banner, the first to have a motto in Irish, was dedicated by the Rev. Martin Smyth who said its emblem "exemplified the movement's belief in the dignity of Irish history".[15] They spoke of "a tendency of a section of the Protestant people in Northern Ireland to ... consider themselves solely as Ulstermen and Britishers".[16] A newspaper account said of them, "they were proud to be Irish and they want to emphasise the Protestant part of the Irish heritage".[17]

More importantly, mentioning the 'Erin go Bragh' over the pavilion in Botanic Park for the Ulster Unionist Convention of 1892, McGimpsey adverts to the 1882 letter quoted by Cathal O'Byrne and says:

> I believe that many Irishmen and women of the Unionist tradition are not prepared to let that happen here [the death of the language] and are, in fact, prepared to endorse the Irish language.

In this, he was endorsing the observations of Risteárd Ó Glaisne, the Methodist author of many books in Irish, who said:

> The still highly persistent strain in Irish life is its most distinctive one, and, I think, the most interesting ... I won't remind you, fellow Protestants, that the Gaelic revival of the last two centuries has its roots in the Belfast Harp Festival of 1791, a festival of mainly Protestant patronage.[18]

"At its height ... the Gaelic League had successfully crossed all the dividing lines of class and creed in Ireland," said Dr. Donal Caird.[19] The aspirations and hopes of the movement may again, can again, hopefully will again do so.

The Belfast born Presbyterian minister and lecturer in Irish at Trinity College Dublin, Terence McCaughey has written:

> It should go without saying that repudiation of a specific culture is a poor response to the realisation that Christianity must never allow itself to be linked exclusively to any one cultural/linguistic expression. For the fact is, that it is only in and through a specific culture that the faith can ever be transmitted and lived at all. This is not just an unfortunate accident. A particular language and culture is not the disposable wrapper in which culture or religion are parcelled; it is their symbolic medium, infinitely precious and each time unique. Imperial powers recognise this in a grudging way every time they try to replace the native language of a subject by their own.[20]

John Robb gave me a typescript of a talk he gave in the early 90s. In this talk, he said:

> Time and devotion rather than impatience and dictation will ensure the survival of the Gaelic language and if this attitude can be inculcated then, as sure as day follows night, as Northern Protestants search for their real roots in the history about which so many of them seem to know so little, they could paradoxically become the torch-bearers of a fresh interest in the Gaelic heritage which has, for one reason or another, been so casually denied to them for so long.

Professor Simon Lee said at the Opsahl Commission hearings:

> The Irish language, for instance, is mistakenly attributed to one team ... we all grow if linguistic or other rights are safeguarded.[21]

Earlier editions of the present work, rights being so much in our minds then, concluded:

> Is it not a civil right of all the people of Northern Ireland, Protestant and Catholic, that they have access, in education at least,

to all that belongs in their heritage, to its folklore and music, to its literature and song, and to the Irish language—the key, the kernel and the keeper of so much of it? I hope that this sketch has given some indication that the Irish language stratum is a deep and a significant one in the hidden heritage of the Ulster Protestant.

More attention has been paid to this in the meantime. There is a deepening awareness that Irish is no longer as 'foreign' a concept as it was for many. The foundation in 1989 of Iontaobhas ULTACH "to widen the appreciation of the Irish language and culture throughout the community in Northern Ireland", is a recognition and one must wish it well, including its Protestant members, Dr. Ian Adamson, Leslie Burnett, Barry Kinghan, Dr. Chris McGimpsey and Maolcholaim Scott.[22]

If this is to be taken as the augury of a new beginning more, of course, is needed if it is to be successful—much more—in love commitment, dedication, action, and for once one can safely say talk, talk, talk and more talk still—in Irish!

Go dtaga san—agus go luath.

APPENDIX

A Note on Education

Despite Tudor ambivalence as regards Irish (exemplified most during the reign of Queen Elizabeth I), despite vacillation under the Tudors, and despite the long roll of distinguished opponents to the policy of anglicisation (from Bedell, William, Marsh and King onwards), the policy of government—whether inconsistently, viciously or inadequately implemented—and by extension, the general practice of the Established Church, was one of antipathy to the Irish language.

The Presbyterian community in Ireland, though for long suffering under penal disabilities imposed by the state and by the established church[1], "brought with it popular schools fashioned after the Scottish Model".[2] What little evidence there is, from the County Down[3], indicates that these schools were, except for those of the Neilson family, English medium schools, and thus in their own way were a contributing factor to the language shift to English in Ulster.[4] Certainly, at least, this was the pattern in Scotland, and it followed on legislation at the inception of the Dual Kingdom.[5]

The first mark there of hostility to Gaelic was perhaps the Act of 1609 for the suppression of the bards, with the concurrent act expecting of every laird and gentleman that he send his eldest child south "to receive an English and Protestant Education".[6] Subsequent legislation reinforced this bias; the 1616 Act of Privy Council "in favour of the universal planting of the English language and the abolition and removal of the Irish language in the Highland and Islands", an act confirmed by the Scottish Parliament in 1631 and succeeded by the Statute of Iona in 1646 encouraging the setting up of an English language school in every Highland parish.[7] There is no doubt but that then also "the first attitude of the education authorities was deliberately antagonistic to Gaelic and directly aimed at destroying the language", as was said of a later period in Scottish history.[8]

James I, who in July 1605 disabused his Catholic subjects of the illusion "that we would allow them liberty of conscience"[9], while disparaging Irish itself did continue the provision that TCD train Irish-speaking clergy.[10] But neither in his time nor later was any provision made in Glasgow University for the training in Irish (or indeed Scots) of candidates for the Presbyterian ministry.[11]

In certain parts of Scotland, the policy of anglicisation through the schools seemed to have continued uninterruptedly. This is suggested, for example, by the programmes of the schools in Ayrshire[12], though there is evidence that teachers may have had to be able to communicate with monoglot pupils: a 1762 advertisement for a schoolmaster in Barr expected this of the candidates[13].

In 1650, the Synod of Argyll declared that:

> Because the knowledge of the English language is so necessary for the weall of the Gospell, the Scriptures not being translated in Irish ... use be made of poor boys that can read and speak English in the interim till schools be erected.[14]

A major force against the indigenous language was the Society for the Propagation of Christian Knowledge, founded with the support of Queen Anne, in 1709. Its

> ... general object was to erect and maintain schools in such parts of the Highlands and Islands of Scotland, as should be thought to need them most; in which schools the children of Popish as well as Protestant parents, should be taught the English language, reading and writing and especially the principles of true religion.[15]

The Society's policy here was, initially at any rate, counter to that of the church in many areas. In the early 18th century "The Church had thought it expedient to subsidise Gaelic-speaking Divinity students". In 1708, the Aberdeen Presbytery encouraged "Students having the Irish language".[16] An SPCK teacher in 1713 fell "under the Society's displeasure because he proposed printing the Catechism in Gaelic". In 1722, they stated their "object was to extirpate Gaelic", and, in 1725, the Society urged its Committee "to prosecute the former motions concerning the more Speedy extirpating of the Irish language".[17]

In 1753, noting the "great disadvantages arising from allowing scholars to Speak Irish", they forbade pupils "either in the Schoolhouse, or when playing about the Doors thereof, to speak Erse, under the pain of being Chastised, and that Schoolmasters appoint Censors to note down and report to them such as Transgress this Rule".[18] In effect, as Campbell, John Lorne Campbell says concerning the SPCK:

> For two generations ... they had prostituted what is supposed to be one of the fundamental principles of the Protestantism they professed, viz., that every man shall have the opportunity of searching the Scriptures in his own language.[19]

Elsewhere, Campbell compares their schools "with the German schools ... set up in Poland by Bismarck to attack Polish traditions and language".[20] Stung, however by reproaches such as Samuel Johnson's famous letter, in which he wrote:

> Their language is attacked on every side. Schools are erected in which English only is taught, and there were lately some who thought it reasonable to refuse them ... the Holy Scriptures that they might have no monument of their mother tongue ...

The society changed its policy somewhat and compiled and produced the New Testament in Gaelic in 1767 [21] and removed its ban on teaching and reading in Gaelic.[22] Some of the Presbyteries did not take too kindly to this change of policy[23], but "the prejudice against Gaelic largely disappeared in the 19th century"[24], by which time, however, the decline of the Gaeltacht in Scotland had become very, very marked, something which leads Simpson to comment: "If, however, those schools played a part in the depopulation of the Highlands, and if their hostility to Gaelic helped to destroy an ancient culture, their establishment was a mixed blessing."[25]

Campbell writes of two phases concerning Gaelic. The first was marked by the "abuse which the extreme Presbyterian party ... poured upon Gaelic and its associations during the 17th and 18th centuries"; and the second "begins about 1760, when Jacobitism was no longer felt to be a danger to the Government" and "During this time the Established Church tolerates the teaching of Gaelic, at any rate for the purpose of imparting religious instruction and some of its clergy attain a considerable Gaelic scholarship, but the State is still hostile"[26]—as the 1872 Education Act underlined. It was not until the 1918 Education Act that any state provision for the teaching of Gaelic in Gaelic-speaking areas was made.[27]

It was, interestingly enough, in the mid 18th century also that churchmen began "to make provision for the majority for whom it [Gaelic] was the only effective means of communication" in Man, in contradistinction to 17th-century attitudes such as that of Bishop Barrow who "had already concluded that the cure for Manx ignorance and slackness in religious matters was to teach the inhabitants English"; and in opposition to the continued attitude of "those geniuses of the South, who think the cultivation of that language *unnecessary*", such as the Manx grammarian, John Kelly, who wrote in 1805, "when there shall be one national language, then only wi the union of the empire be completely established".[28]

One of the most interesting examples of the changed attitude in the 19th century, which Ian J. Simpson mentioned[29],—at a period when Irish was very much neglected in Maynooth College[30]—was Dr. Norman Mac Leod, who at one stage of his career ministered "to the Gaelic congregation in Glasgow"; and who, when developing an educational plan, "waited upon the Roman Catholic Bishop ... explained to him at great length the nature of our education scheme, assuring him that our schools should always be open to Roman Catholic priests, and that the catechism of the Church of Scotland would not be forced on Roman Catholic children, nor any books disapproved of by them", preached, wrote and published consistently in Gaelic; and as a result of "representations made and the encouragement given to him by the Synod of Ulster" produced the Irish "metrical version of the Psalms of David for the use of the Church of Ireland".[31] *Si sic omnes sint.*

Notes & Index

CHAPTER ONE
A Heritage denied

[1] Blackstaff, 1974 edn., p.198

[2] F. Collinson, *The Traditional and National Music of Scotland*, London, *1966, p.*230.

[3] [4] *loc. cit.* 129, 130.

[5] *ibid.*

[6] pp.130, 131

[7] p.131

[8] *ibid.*

[9] Crone, *National Biography, p.189*

[10] Purser, pp.11, 15, 16, 19. In discussing later music, such as Donal Fraser's 19th Century *An Nighean Donn na Buaile* and a ploughing tune based on the *caoine*, he refers to the probable influence of Irish immigrants (pp.232, 235).

[11] Even to the memory of the Irish harper McIlvenny at Queen's Island and later Ormeau Park ('Memories of Queen's Island', by 'Odd Man', *Belfast Evening Telegraph* 22nd April 1905) and even to the echoes of some Irish and Oirish (tin pan alley version) airs being the tunes for many of John McKeague's collection of Loyalist ballads, *Orange Loyalist Songbook*, Belfast, 1971. (McKeague is an anglicization of Mac Thaidhg which could be translated as "Taig's son"). What is 'Boyne Water' in Ulster is 'Rosc Catha na Mumhan' elsewhere.

[12] Richard Rose cites Coupland, as to "the aggressive policy of Anglicization by the British Government in Welsh and Irish schools in the 19th century", in his study *The United Kingdom as a Multi-National State*, Strathclyde, (2nd printing) 1973 p.10.

[13] *Rosc*, March, 1971, p.3. P. Ó Fearaíl, *The Story of Conradh na Gaeilge*, Dublin, 1975, p.21.

[14] Rev. J.G. Mac Manaway, *Partition Why Not?*, (n.d., c. 1948), p.4.

[15] A and O being in almost the exactly opposite proportions to those which obtain in England! cf. Mourant and Kopek, *The ABO Groups* .

[16] c. 1,000 in Belfast directories and c. 1,400 in the Dublin ones for 1858. Of course many, many, surnames hid the Gaelic root and "the Mac and O" is a very rough criterion indeed.

[17] Mac Neill, *Phases of Irish History*, Dublin, 1919, p.5. Purser, *op. cit.*, p.130.

[18] Even to the B&ICO's ludicrous slogan 'Culture Divides Workers, We Want Unity!' on some of their publications.

[19] Cf. the data in the Irish Free State Government's *Handbook of the Ulster Question*, Dublin, 1923, especially the chapter headed 'The Two Nations theory.' (Kevin R. O'Shiel was, most likely, its author).

[20] Self-styled. cf. J. Lane 'Socialism and Nationalism', *The Irish Communist*, July, 1971, p.1.

[21] In an article 'Hidden Ulster Revisited' (*The Crane Bag*, Vol. 5, no. 2, p.46). I mentioned their attacks on *Hidden Ulster* and that they published an attempted rebuttal (*Hidden Ulster Explored*—unsigned but written by Rosamund Mitchell) which insofar as it pinpointed weaknesses in the earlier printings of *Hidden Ulster* was taken into account in the 1977 edition.

[22] B&ICO, *The Irish Language: Revivalism and the Gaeltacht*, Belfast, May 1972, pp.1-14.

[23] *Present State of Ireland*, London (publ. Wilkinson), 1673, p.xi.

[24] 'An Irish Protestant Culture' in J. McLoone, ed., *Being Protestant in Ireland*, Belfast and Dublin, 1985, p.72.

[25] Something which could survive the Penal Laws themselves as in a Farney estate where the practice was not to give vacated farms to Catholics whenever possible (Tomás Mac Ardail, 'Buachaillí Fhearnmhaí' in Peadar Ó Casaide, ed., *Énrí Ó Muirgheasa (1874-1945)* Carrickmacross (?), n.d. (? 1974), p.25).

[26] Andy Pollak, ed., *A Citizen's Inquiry: The Opsahl Report*, Dublin, 1993, p.96.

[27] Ian R.K. Paisley MP, MEP, *The Pope is the Antichrist ... Being a Precis of Dr. J.A. Wylie's Classic 'The Papacy is the Antichrist'*, Belfast, n.d. Cf. also Anthony Buckley, 'We're trying to find our identity: Uses of history among Ulster Protestants' in Tonkin, McDonald and Chapman, *History and Ethnicity*, London and New York, 1989, p. 190.

CHAPTER TWO
Languages of the Plantation

[1] J. Braidwood, 'Ulster and Elizabethan English' in G.B. Adams, ed., *Ulster Dialects* (Cultra, 1964, p.6)

[2] cf. the *Dictionary of the Older Scottish Tongue* for the essential points of differentiation between these two languages and their separate roots. See also Hugh Mac Diarmid, *Lucky Poet* (London, 1972, p.387) and Withers, *op. cit.*, p. 23.

[3] *Featsa*, Meitheamh-Iúil, 1972, p.2 (based on data from the Ulster Dialect Archives).

[4] G.B. Adams, 'The Last Language Census in Northern Ireland', *Ulster Dialects*, p.140.

[5] Braidwood, *op. cit.*, p.19.

[6] *Down's Angelic Genius (Aodh Mac Aingil)*, Newry, n.d., pp.5, 6.

[7] A. Mac Póilín, *The Protestant Gaelic Tradition, Iontaobhas ULTACH*, Belfast, n.d., p.2. Dunkin is placed in context—he had been a curate in Creggan in Armagh and a friend to Ussher—in Risteárd Giltrap, *An Ghaeilge in Eaglais na hÉireann*, Dublin, 1990, pp.21-23.

[8] B&ICO, *op. cit.*, p.40. Almost certainly one of the sources of their 'two nations' theory is M.W. Heslinga, a Dutch geographer, who says in his book, *The Irish Border as a Cultural Divide* (Assen, Nederlands, 1962), p.193, that "the great majority of Protestants never spoke the language" (a view with which Deirdre Ní Fhlannagáin concurs in '*Scoti agus Ulster Scots*', *An tUltach*, May, 1970). Heslinga, whose book was re-issued at the instigation of NUM (whose then treasurer undertook to publicise the first edition of the present work, but failed signally to honour that undertaking), also said however (*op. cit.*, p.159):

> As far as the language is concerned, there was no clear-cut division between the immigrants and the 'natives'. It is fairly certain that many colonists of the first three decades of the seventeenth century who came from Galloway were Gaelic speakers. The same holds good for the (later) immigrants from the Highlands whose descendants in some cases, remained Gaelic-speaking until the first half of the nineteenth century.

Heslinga also refers to the existance of native Irish-speaking Protestants, followers of "some of the lesser Gaelic chiefs, especially in East Ulster" and cites Adams, ('The Emergence of Ulster as a Distinct Dialect Area', *Ulster Folklife*, 1958, pp.68/9) concerning "several population groups" of Irish-speakers and who—he suggests—"tended to become first bilingual and monoglot English-speaking at an earlier date (than) the main body of Gaelic-speakers."

[9] G.B. Adams, *Ulster Dialects*, pp.xiv, 1-4.

[10] Domhnuill Iain Mac Aoidh, president of An Comunn Gaidhealach, speaking in Edinburgh on 11th February, 1966. Tension existed, of course, between both languages as witness the 'Flyting' of Dunbar (from Lothian) and Kennedy from Galloway c.1505 where Kennedy says

> Thou lufis nane Irische, elf, I understand,
> Bot it suld be all trew Scottis mennis lede;
> It was the gud language of this land,
> And Scotia it causit to multiply and sprede

in reply to Dunbar's criticism. (I am indebted to Aodán Mac Póilín for this reference.)

[11] H. J. Paton, *The Claim of Scotland*, London, 1968, pp.215, 216.

[12] J. Braidwood, *The Ulster Dialect Lexicon*, Belfast, 1969, p.4.

[13] *ibid.*, p.34.

[14] For a further comment on Scots as a separate language cf. Robert Burns' comment "I have not that command of the (English) language that I have of my own native tongue" (p.558, *The Complete Poetical Works of Robert Burns with an Appreciation by Lord Rosebery*). Burns of course showed no hostility to and a certain familiarity with Gaelic, as witness the lines:

> Wad ding a Lallan tongue, or Erse,
> In prose or rhyme
> —'Address to the Deil'
> And in his freaks had 'luath' ca'd him,
> After some dog in Highland sang,
> —'The Twa Dogs'
> Blest highland bonnet! Once my proudest dress,
> How prouder still, Maria's temples press ...
> I see her face the first of Ireland's sons,
> and even out-Irish his Hibernian bronze
> —'Epistle from Esopus to Maria'

Textbooks were needed which "enabled English to be taught to Scots almost as if it were a foreign tongue" (H.J. Hanham, *Scottish Nationalism*, London, 1969, p.35). Sneers at the London court are said to have impelled James VI to ever more anti-Scots attitudes. Cf also fn 11 p. 131 *infra.*

[15] John A. McIvor, *Popular Education in the Presbyterian Church,* Dublin, 1969, p.81.

[16] Risteárd Ó Glaisne, *The Irish Language, A Protestant Speaks to His Co-Religionists,* Dublin, 1965, p.6.

[17] Mrs. C.V. Warke, private communication, 19th August 1994.

[18] *Cuisle na hÉigse,* Newry, 1993, p.79.

[19] *The Opsahl Report,* p.341

[20] 'Can Unionists endorse the Irish language', typescript of a speech delivered in Kilkenny on 25th February 1993.

[21] P.L. Henry, 'Anglo-Irish Word Charts', *Ulster Dialects,* p.148.

[22] Eoin Mac Neill, *op. cit.,* p.p.220, 221, (1968 edn.). W. Power, *Wallace Monument: The Official Guide. Encyclopædia Britannica,* 1950 edn.,vol. xx, p.312. R. Nicholson 'Sequel to Edward Bruce's Invasion of Ireland', *Scottish Historical Review,* vol. 42, 1962, pp.38, 39. R. Frame, 'The Bruces in Ireland 1315-18', *Irish Historical Studies,* March 1974, p.45.

[23] *Presbyterians and the Irish Language,* Belfast, forthcoming. Cf. also Ian Adamson, 'The Ulster-Scottish Connection', in Ian S. Wood, ed., *Scotland and Ulster,* Edinburgh, 1994, pp.5-10. For some modification of this presentation cf C.W.J. Withers, *Gaelic in Scotland 1698-1981,* Edinburgh, 1984, pp. 18-23.

[24] P.L. Henry, *loc. cit.* Cf. also G.A. Hayes McCoy, *Scottish Mercenary Forces in Ireland,* Dublin, 1937.

[25] R.A. Stradling, *The Spanish Monarchy and Irish Mercenaries,* Dublin, 1994, pp.60, 61.

[26] Adamson, *op. cit.,* p.9.

[27] Rev. James O'Laverty, M.R.I.A., *An Historical Account of the Diocese of Down and Connor, Ancient and Modern,* Dublin, 1878, pp.6, 7.

[28] Eleanor Knott, ed., *The Bardic Poems of Tadhg Dall Ó Huiginn (1550-1591),* Vol. I, London, 1922, p.xxiii.

[29] Knott, *op. cit.,* vol.I, p.p.173-179; vol.II, London, 1926, pp.115-119, 264-266.

[30] Magnus Mac Lean, *The Literature of the Celts,* Glasgow, 1902, e.g. pp.119, 126, 129-133, 276.

[31] *Alasdair Mac Colla,* Clódhanna Teoranta, 1914. Laoide (Lloyd's) father had been a member of the Society for the Preservation of the Irish Language and for years, before the decline of Clódhanna Teo.

(the Gaelic League's publishing imprint), Laoide was their dynamo. For a nice appreciation of his sad life cf. Henry Morris 'A Forgotten Patriot' in *Macalla*, 2, 1977, pp.23-29.

[32] Anraí Mac Giolla Chomhaill, ed., *Díolaim Próis 1450-1850*, Dublin, 1971, pp.125-127. At least four of the prose items here are Protestant by provenance and/or authorship.

[33] Mairghréad Nic Philibín, ed., *Na Casadaigh agus a gCuid Filidheachta*, Dublin, 1936, p.36.

[34] Uilleam Mac Giolla Íosa, (Dept. of Celtic, University of Edinburgh), private communication, 9th June 1973.

[35] Henry, *op. cit., loc. cit.*

[36] *House of Commons Journal*, May 1615.

[37] Charles Forman, *A Defence of the Courage, Honour, and Loyalty of the Irish Nation ...*, Dublin, 1747, p.4.

[38] 'From Uladh to Galloway and from Galloway to Uladh,' *The Red Hand Magazine*, Vol. 1, no. 3, November, 1920, p.22.

[39] E. Estyn Evans, *Irish Folk Ways*, London, 1967, p.8.

[40] 'Cultural Connection in North-West Britain and Ireland', in *Ethnologia Europa*, vol. ii-iii, p.139.

[41] *Folklore of the Ulster People*, Cork, 1971, p.7.

[42] e.g. D.C. Rushe, *History of Monaghan for 200 Years 1660-1860*, Dundalk, 1921, p.p.25-6. Aodh de Blácam, 'The Other Hidden Ireland' (whence the subtitle of this book), *Studies*, September, 1934, p.433. See also P. Mac Con Midhe, 'Gaeilge an Dúin,' *An tUltach*, December, 1968. Padruig Mac Gille-Domhnaich computed that 80 per cent were "of Scottish-Gaelic origin",'The Scottish Settlers in Ulster', *The Red Hand*, Vol. 1, no. 4, p.6.

[43] Mac Con Midhe, *op. cit.*

[44] Brian Ó Cuív, *Irish Dialects and Irish-speaking Districts*, Dublin, 1971, p.15.

[45] Cathaldus Giblin, O.F.M., *Irish Franciscan Mission to Scotland, 1619-1646*, Dublin 1964.

[46] Donald Buchanan, *Reflections on the Isle of Barra*, London 1942, pp.90-93.

[47] Denis Kennedy, 'Foreword' to T.M. Healy, *The Great Fraud of Ulster*, Tralee, 1971, p.5.

[48] Kennedy, *op. cit.,* p.12.

[49] Rev. Geo. Hill, *An Historical Account of the Plantation in Ulster at the Commencement of the Seventeenth Century 1608-1620*, Belfast, 1877, p.73.

[50] *ibid.*

[51] M. Perceval-Maxwell, *The Scottish Migration to Ulster in the Reign of James I*, London, 1973, p.114.

[52] T. F. O'Rahilly, *Irish Dialects Past and Present*, Dublin 1972, pp.161-164.

[53] O'Rahilly, *op. cit*, p.163. W.L. Lorimer, 'The Persistence of Gaelic in Galloway and Carrick', *Scottish Gaelic Studies*, VI (1949) and VII (1953).

[54] T.J. Barron, 'Rev. Alexander Mc Whidd; A Seventeenth Century Minister in Knockbride, Co. Cavan', *Breifne*, Vol. 1, no. 2, p.155.

[55] *The Earl of Castlehaven's Memoirs; or, his Review of the Civil Wars in Ireland ...*, Dublin, 1815, p.134.

[56] O'Rahilly, *op. cit.,* pp.117, 140. G. B. Adams, 'Ulster as a Distinct Dialect Area',*Ulster Folklife*, Vol. 4 (1958), p.69.

[57] W. J. Watson, *Bardachd Ghaidhlig*, Inverness, 1918, p.xxi.

[58] A. Archibald, letters to me, October, 1972.

[59] William Boyd, *Education in Ayrshire through Seven Centuries*, London, 1961, p.3. Withers, *op. cit.*, p. 38 attempts to derogate from Lorimer *et al* on this point but that section of his valuable study is stronger on assertion than it is on fact: it ignores, for example, Boyd's factual evidence given here—it doesn't even list his book (essential reading on the topic) in the bibliography or index.

[60] P. Ó Snodaigh, 'Hidden Ulster Revisited', *The Crane Bag*, Vol. 5, no.2, 1980, p.46. Withers, *op. cit.*, p. 57.

[61] R.de B. Trotter, 'Highland Troops in the Southwest in 1715 and 1745',*Galloway Gossip*, Kirkudbrightshire, 1901, p.108. (I am indebted to Adam Busby for this reference.)

[62] 'Fionn Mac Colla', *Ro Fhada Mar Seo A Tha Mi*, Thurso, 1975, p.58.

[63] Perceval-Maxwell, *op. cit.*, p.105. For Gaelic in Stirlingshire in the 19th Century cf. Withers, pp. 307, 321; and in Banff, Aberdeen, and Angus in the 18th and 19th centuries cf. Withers, pp. 207, 308, 311. The bellows of the anti-Catholic riots of 1780, Lord George of the Berwick Gordons, though born in London, educated at Eton, and sometimes resident of Edinburgh, was a Gaelic speaker—cf *.DNB* and Christopher Hibbert, *King Mob*, London, 1959, p. 31.

[64] *ibid.*

[65] *op. cit.*, p.104.

[66] p.120

[67] p.121.

68 p.155.
69 p.190.
70 p.204.
71 p.313.
72 Adams, *op. cit., loc. cit.*
73 Adams to me, January 1975.
74 Adams, *op. cit., loc. cit.*, Dunseverick, Ballintoy, Ballycastle, Fairhead, Camlough and Portballantrae are likely areas for these migrations.
75 Eoghan Ó Néill, *Gleann an Óir*, Dublin, 1988, p.5.
76 Maolcholaim Scott, 'Where the Planter was the Gael', *Fortnight* 316, 'Ballymascanlon and Irish Links with Gaelic Scotland', *Cuisle na nGael* Newry, no. 7, 1991, pp.132, 133.

CHAPTER THREE
The Irish Language and Ulster Protestantism

1 Adams, 'The Emergence of Ulster as a Distinct Dialect Area', *Ulster Folklife*, 4, 1958, p.68. For the primacy being English cf. the useful overview by Giltrap, *op. cit.*, p.29.
2 *State Papers Henry VIII*, Vol. 3, part 3, (1834), p.306.
3 Mac Neill, *op. cit.*, pp.6,7.
4 Cf. Pádraig Mac Giolla Domhnaigh's *Some Ulster Surnames*, Clódhanna, Dublin, 1975—a reprint of a pamphlet originally published earlier this century .
5 Énrí Ó Muirgheasa, *Céad de Cheoltaibh Uladh*, Dublin, 1915, p.p.148-151. Modern authorities do not agree with Ó Muirgheasa's identification of the writer, though all concur in taking him to have been English.
6 Brian Ó Cuív, 'The Changing Form of the Irish Language', in *A View of the Irish Language*, Dublin, 1969, p.25. J. S. Reid, *History of the Presbyterian Church in Ireland*, vol. 1, Belfast, 1867, pp.35, 51-53, Mac Neill, *op. cit.*, pp.6, 7.
7 F.R. Bolton, *The Caroline Tradition of the Church of Ireland*, London, 1968, p.3.

[8] In James McLoone, ed., *op. cit.*, p.72.

[9] Pádraig Ó Mearáin, citing Colles in his article 'Sracamharc ar Stair Charraig Mhachaire Rois', in Peadar Ó Casaide, ed., *op. cit.*, p.47.

[10] 'The Political Background to the Ulster Plantation, 1607-1620', in Brian Mac Cuarta, ed., *Ulster 1641: Aspects of the Rising*, Belfast, 1993, p.22.

[11] *op. cit.*, p.27.

[12] 'The O'Kane Papers', presented by A.F.O.D. Alexander, *Analecta Hibernica*, no.12, 1943. The distinction between English and Scots is interesting: so many have failed to make it.

[13] Dr. Wyse Jackson, in Cosslett Ó Cuinn, ed., *Scéalta as an Apocrypha*, Dublin, 1971, p.10.

[14] Bolton, *op. cit.*, p.7.

[15] Deasún Breatnach, *Bedell and the Irish Version of the Old Testament*, Clódhanna, Dublin, 1971, p.6.

[16] Aodh de Blácam, *A First Book of Irish Literature*, pp.129, 147.

[17] Kearns, *op. cit.*, p.39.

[18] Breatnach, *op. cit.*, pp.7, 8. W. Gamble, *William Bedell, His Life and Times*, n.d. (?1951), n.p., p.32.

[19] Jackson, *op. cit.*, p.12. Breatnach, *op. cit.*, p.8.

[20] Breatnach, *op. cit.*, p.12, Cosslett Quin in Pilib Mistéil, ed., *op. cit.*, p.31.

[21] Jackson, *op. cit.*, p.p.18-21. Séamus Mac Cnáimhín, *Éireannaigh San Eolaíocht*, Dublin, 1966, pp.17. R. E. W. Maddison, *The Life of the Honourable Robert Boyle, FRS*, London, 1969, p.141. R. Ó Glaisne, 'Irish and the Protestant Tradition', *The Crane Bag*, Vol. 5, no. 2, 1981, p.35.

[22] Breatnach, *op. cit.*, p.2. A Mac Póilín, *The Protestant Gaelic Tradition*, Iontaobhas ULTACH, Belfast, n.d., p.1.

[23] Breatnach, *op. cit.*, p.11. For an account of one of his clergy, Alexander McWhidd, cf. Barron, *op. cit.*, pp.11, 12.

[24] Bolton, *op. cit.*, p.16. Jackson, *op. cit.*, pp.11, 12. Ó Glaisne, *op. cit.*, p.34.

[25] Breatnach, *op. cit.*, p.7. Giltrap, *op. cit.*, p.23 refers to Murdo McKenzy preaching in Irish in mid-century.

[26] Énrí Ó Muirgheasa, *Dhá Chéad de Cheoltaibh Uladh*, Dublin, 1969, p.16. 'Filíocht Chúige Uladh', in P. Ó Fiannachta, ed., *Léachtaí Cholm Cille*, XIII, Maynooth, 1982, p.179.

[27] 'The Emergence of Ulster as a Distinct Dialect Area', *Ulster Folklife*, vol. 4, (1858), pp.68, 69.

[28] Ó Muirgheasa, *loc. cit.* Mac Póilín, *op. cit.*, p.1.

[29] Ó Cuív, *Irish Dialects* ..., p.17.

[30] *op. cit.*, pp.16, 17.

[31] Bolton, *op. cit.*, p.40.

[32] W. Alison Phillips, ed., *History of the Church of Ireland*, Vol. 3, London, 1933, p.136.

[33] Philips, *op. cit.*, p.137.

[34] Ó Cuív, *op. cit.*, pp.18, 19.

[35] John Richardson, *A Proposal for the Conversion of the Popish Natives of Ireland to the Established Religion*, 1711, p.14. Duncan Mac Arthur, Archibald Stewart and Archibald McCollum are among the names mentioned by Richardson. For Rasharkin cf. H. Mac Neill, *The Annals of the Parish of Derrykeighan* (1910) and Cahal Dallat's use of it in 'Some Notes on the Fullertons', *Ulster Local Studies*, Vol. 16, No.2., Winter 1994, pp.38-39. For Richardson see the sections from his *Short History* ... (London, 1713, pp.28-30) in Colmán Ó Huallacháin, *The Irish Language in Society*, Coleraine, 1991, pp. 105-106. Mac Neill's pamphlet was republished, with an introduction by Dr. Eull Dunlop, in Ballymena in 1993.

[36] Phillips, *op. cit.*, pp.188, 189. J.S. Reid, *History of the Presbyterian Church in Ireland*, Vol. iii, Belfast, 1867, p.9.

[37] Phillips, *op. cit.*, p.166. Reid, *op. cit.*, *loc. cit.* David Greene, 'The Irish Language Movement', in M. Hurley, ed., *Irish Anglicanism 1869-1969*, Dublin, 1970, p.110.

[38] Bolton, *op. cit.*, p.47.

[39] Ó Cuív, *op. cit.*, p.19.

[40] Bolton, *op. cit.*, p.155.

[41] Anna Heusaff, *Filí agus Cléir san Ochtú Aois Déag*, Dublin 1992, p.41.

[42] Phil Kilroy, 'Protestantism in Ulster, 1610-1641', in Mac Cuarta, *op. cit.*, p.27. For a study of one such mobile, the Fermanagh born sometime Bishop of Down and Connor, Myler Mc Grath, see Odhrán Ó Duáin, *Rógaire Easpaig*, Dublin, 1975.

[43] Cf. the accounts of Spottiswood in Clogher, in Kilroy, *op. cit.*, p.30.

[44] Alan Harrison, *John Toland (1670-1722) Béal Eiriciúil as Inis Eoghain*, Dublin, 1994. Also T. C. Barnard, 'Protestants and the Irish Language c. 1675-1725', *Journal of Ecclesiatical History*, Vol. 44, no. 2, April 1993, p.271.

[45] Crone, *op. cit.*, p.144. *DNB*, xii, pp.728, 729.

[46] Seán de Rís, *Peadar Ó Doirnín*, Dublin, 1969, pp.xii, xiii, xx, 90, 91,

103. Johnson of the Fews—another Ó Doirnín contact—was also an Irish speaker (M.J. Murphy, Radio Éireann talk, 20th May 1972.)

47 De Blácam, 'The Other Hidden Ireland', *loc. cit.*, pp.447, 448.

48 Séamus Ó Casaide 'The Irish Language in Belfast and Co. Down, AD 1601— AD 1850', *Down and Connor Historical Society Journal*, Belfast, 1929, p.6. *Transaction of the Iberno-Celtic Society for 1820*, Vol. 1, pp.ccvciv, cxvcv.

49 Breandán Ó Buachalla, 'Arthur Brownlow: A Gentleman more Curious than Ordinary', *Ulster Local Studies*, Vol. 7, no. 2, 1982 (?), pp.24-28.

50 'The Last Language Census in Northern Ireland', G.B. Adams, *Ulster Dialects*, Cultra, 1964, p.138.

51 Ó Buachalla, *op. cit.*, p.26. The Iontaobhas ULTACH brochure *The Protestant Gaelic Tradition*, (p.2) points out, however, that Brownlow did in fact replace Irish Catholic tenants with English. All is ambiguity! Certainly there are no hard and fast lines in all this—as in most of Irish history. Anna Heusaff, *op. cit*, p.19 cites Corish to the effect that "Society in 18th century Ireland was organised on the assumption that Catholics ... were an inferior class ... [a] notion, the product of more than a century of misrepresentation ... was widely held by Protestants who used it to justify and retain an elaborate code of laws designed to constrict and control 'Popery' rather than to destroy it". Eirenic gestures carry more weight in the context.

52 Ó Glaisne, R., 'Irish and the Protestant Tradition', *The Crane Bag*, Vol. 5, no. 2, 1981, p.37.

53 S. P. Ó Mórdha, 'Údar Tóruidheacht na bhFireun ar Lorg Chríosda', *Studia Hibernica*, 1963, p.171.

54 Breandán Ó Buachalla, *I mBéal Feirste Cois Cuain*, Dublin 1968, pp.12, 13. Irish was still the main language on Rathlin until well into the 19th century—Wallace Clarke, *Rathlin, Disputed Island*, Portlaw, 1971, p.35.

55 R.A. Breatnach, 'The End of a Tradition', *Studia Hibernica*, 1961, p.143.

56 PRONI, D.3577/3A. Hutchinson is asking about a new alphabet and also addressed the political aspect of the undertaking. "As to your political Objection from the danger of strengthening the Irish nation so as to make greater head against ye English I meddle not with it. Our Business is to save mens souls ... I never have any fear of doing harm by doing my duty; nor have I any fear but the wisdom of the two

Nations will find a way to preserve that Union which even Nature by the Situation of the two Nations, hath made necessary for both." Cf. also Colm Ó Baoill, 'Norman Mac Leod—Cara na nGael', *Scottish Gaelic Studies*, Vol. XIII, pt. II, Summer 1981, p.167, f.n. 6, for a reference to unpublished Irish versions—probably in Hutchinson's experimental phonetics—of 6 of the psalms prepared for that bishop of Down and Connor.

[57] Barnard, *op. cit.*, p.254.

[58] *ibid.*

[59] Ó Glaisne, *op. cit.*, p.35.

[60] Barnard, *op. cit.* pp.254, 255, 258.

[61] p.265.

[62] pp.263-265.

[63] p.272.

[64] Michelle O'Riordan, 'The Native Ulster *mentalité* as revealed in Gaelic Sources 1600-1650', Mac Cuarta, ed., *op. cit.*, p.83.

[65] Raymond Gillespie, 'Destabilizing Ulster 1641-2', Mac Cuarta, ed., *op. cit.*, p.110.

[66] Richardson, *op. cit.*, p.16.

[67] Roger Blayney, in *Presbyterianism and the Irish Language*, Belfast, forthcoming, adds that "This may be James Stuart, minister for Cushendall from 1708 to 1719, who is not elsewhere described as being an Irish speaker."

[68] John A. McIvor, *Extracts from a Ballybay Scrapbook*, Monaghan, 1974, p.19.

[69] Cited by Rev. Cosslett Quin in *Pilib Mistéil*, ed., *op. cit.*, p.30.

[70] 'The Last Language Census in Northern Ireland', Adams, ed., *op. cit.*, p.133.

[71] T.H. Mullin, *Limavady and the Roe Valley*, Limavady, 1983, pp.10, 11.

[72] *Fasti of the Irish Presbyterian Church*, 1951 Reprint, p.115.

[73] Cited in Arthur Mitchell (of the University of South Carolina), ed., history pack *Ireland and the American War of Independence*, Academy Press, Dublin, 1973.

[74] *The Ulster Difficulty*, n. d. (? 1920), Dublin, p.8.

[75] *Belfast Newsletter*, 16th April 1773.

[76] Hereward Senior, *The Fenians and Canada*, Toronto, 1978, p.5 citing P. Guilday, *Life and Times of John England*, New York, 1927, p.7 and J.F. Maguire, *The Irish in America*, London, 1868, p.357.

[77] cf. my article 'The Volunteers of Ireland', *Irish Sword*, Vol. 7, no. 27,

Winter 1965, pp.147-159; W. H. Grattan Flood, *The Story of the Bagpipe*, London, 1911, p.149; and my piece 'Hidden Ulster Revisited', in *The Crane Bag*, Vol. 5, no. 2, 1980, pp.45-47.

[78] *An Abstract of the Laws and Rules of the General Synod of Ulster from June, 15th, 1694, to June 1800*, p.15. Reid, *op. cit.*, p.10 and p.11 where he speaks of seven ministers and three probationers able to preach in Irish.

[79] *An Abstract of the Laws ...*, p.16.

[80] Rushe, *op. cit.*, p.26. Rushe also says "The planters were not so long in changing their language, for it was the special care of the Government and their landlords to Anglicise them, and they succeeded in everything until they tried the religion, in that they failed, for the Ulster Presbyterian refused to conform to the established Church." (He is writing here about the 'planters' from Scotland.) Maclaine was "In his day considered one of the best masters of the Irish language". McConnell's, *Fasti*, p.116, entry 318.

[81] Ó Casaide, *op. cit.*, p.90.

[82] McIvor, *Popular Education ...*, p.89. Ó Casaide, *op. cit.*, p.11. Reid, *op. cit.*, p.91.

[83] McIvor, *op. cit.*, p.90.

[84] H. McIlroy, 'Some Old-Time Presbyterians of Dundalk', *Tempest's Annual*, 1940, p.25, Reid, *op. cit*, p.90.

[85] McIlroy, *op. cit.*, p.90.

[86] Ó Casaide, *op. cit.*, p.11. *Fasti*, p.129, entry 388.

[87] J. Johnston's edition of the *Querist* (Dundalk 1970), pp.147, 148 and 181. Rev. Jackson, *The Bible in Ireland*, Dublin, 1950, p.p.14, 15.

[88] Ó Casaide, *op. cit.*, p.27. F. J. Bigger, 'Samuel Bryson—A Belfast Gaelic Scholar', *County Louth Archeological Journal*, Vol. V, p.61. For Fullerton cf. Cahal Dallat, 'Some Notes on the Fullertons', *Ulster Local Studies*, Vol.16, No.2, Winter 1994, p.38

[89] Seán de Fréine, *The Great Silence*, Dublin, 1965, p.126, citing J.J. Campbell in Moody and Beckett, eds., *Ulster Since 1800—A Social Survey*, London, 1957.

[90] T.J. Barron, 'Irish Popular Education in the Nineteenth Century with special reference to County Cavan'—forthcoming. The late T.J., born a Presbyterian, later a member of the Church of Ireland, showed me the work in progress: I have not seen it in print.

[91] T. Wright, *A History of the Rise and Progress of the People called Quakers in Ireland from the Year 1653 to 1700*, 4th edn. (enlarged by John Rutty),

London, 1811, p.129. W. Glynn, 'Three Derry McLoughlins: Quaker, Protestant and Roman in 1678', *Irish Friends Newsletter*, April, 1979, pp.2-5.

[92] Ó Glaisne, *op. cit.*, p.5. Crone, *op. cit.*, p.200. PRONI has a letter of Ouseley's about the mission in 1837.

[93] Mac Con Midhe, *op. cit.*

[94] *Pilib Mistéil*, ed., *op. cit.*, p.37.

[95] *An tUltach*, February 1979, pp.6-8.

[96] March 1979, pp.6, 7.

[97] June 1979, pp.7-9.

[98] July 1979, pp.16-18.

[99] August 1979, pp.12, 13.

[100] *Presbyterianism and the Irish Language*, Belfast, forthcoming. I am deeply indebted to him for the pre-publication sight of his important book.

[101] Maolcholaim Scott, 'When the Planter was the Gael', *Fortnight* 316, pp.25-27.

[102] *ibid.*

[103] McIvor, *op. cit.*, p.59.

[104] 'The Policy of the Presbyterian Church to the Gaelic Language', *The Christian Irishman*, June, 1965, pp.62, 63.

[105] Ó Glaisne, *op. cit.*, p.6.

[106] R. W. Jackson, *op cit.*, p.15.

[107] Ó Glaisne, op. cit., *loc. cit.* Ó Baoill, *op. cit.*, pp.163-165.

[108] Crone, *op. cit.*, p.166.

[109] Green, *op. cit.*, p.110. Some of the novels of the period are in effect tracts for Bible reading. See, e.g. Charlotte Elizabeth's *Derry—A Tale of the Revolution of 1688*, which while showing some Irish being used within the walls, tends to be ambivalent as regards culture, but projects the city's defenders all through as Irish. (6th edn., London, 1839).

[110] McIvor, *op. cit.*, pp.59, 89, 90. Ó Buachalla, *op. cit.*, p.64. For a full length study of Neilson cf. Ó Saothraí, *An Ministir Gaelach*, Dublin 1992. See also the Down County Museum information sheets *Rev. William Neilson and his Irish Grammar*, Downpatrick, 1992 (text by Roger Blayney) and *The Irish Language in County Down* (text by Ciarán Ó Duibhín), Downpatrick, 1993.

[111] Mac Con Midhe, *op. cit.* Mc Ilroy, *op. cit.*, p.90. Ciarán Ó Duibhín, *Irish in County Down Since 1750*, Cumann Gaelach Leath Chathail,

1991, p.16.

[112] McIvor, *op. cit.*, p.90. For clerics' views hostile to the use or revival of Irish at this time see those of the anglican Rev. John Groves of Errigall-Keragh, Rev. John Graham of Maghera and Rev. Dennis Magrath of Ballymascanlon in Shaw Mason's *A Statistical Account or Parochial Survey of Ireland*, Dublin, 1814-1819 (Vol. 3, pp.160, 161, Vol. 1, p.592, and vol. 2, p.72 respectively).

[113] Ó Duibhín, *op. cit.*, p.16. John Magee, 'The Neilsons of Rademon and Down: Educators and Gaelic Scholars', *Familia—Ulster Genealogical Review*, Vol. 2, no. 4, p.64.

[114] Magee, *op. cit.*, pp.64, 66.

[115] Séamus Ó Saothraí, 'William Neilson, DD, MRIA, 1774-1831', *Meascra Uladh*, pp.80-88; 'Dr. Neilson's Irish Grammar', *Bulletin of the Presbyterian Hibernian Society of Ireland*, Vol. 20, March 1991, pp.5-11.

[116] McIvor, *op. cit.*, p.60.

[117] Quoted by A. Albert Campbell, *Notes on the Literary History of Strabane*, Omagh, 1902, pp.74-75.

[118] Earnán de Blaghd, *Briseadh na Teorann*, Dublin, 1955, p.100.

[119] *Ordnance Survey Letters, Cavan/Leitim*, p.103.

[120] De Blácam, *op. cit*, p.451.

[121] *From the Jungle of Belfast*, Belfast, 1973, p.43.

[122] Ó Duibhín, *op. cit.*, p.24. Séamus Ó Néill, 'The Hidden Ulster: Gaelic Pioneers of the North', *Studies*, Spring 1966, pp.65, 66.

[123] Cf. his *Sixty Years Experience as an Irish Landlord* (1894).

[124] *Ordnance Survey Letters, Cavan/Leitrim*, p.43.

[125] Ó Buachalla, 'An Bíobla i nGlinntí Aontroma', *Feasta*, October, November, December, 1963. Catholic clergy hostility to the preachers could be quite vicious as witness their experience e.g. at the hands of the Rev. William McKeague at Culduff in 1848. (cf the Donegal Outrage reports 7/15/291 in the Irish National Archives: I am indebted to Breandán Mac Suibhne for this reference).

[126] *Ordnance Survey Letters, Down*, p.53.

[127] Ó Casaide, *op. cit.*, p.51. J. Fitzsimons, 'The Official Presbyterian Irish Language Policy in the Eighteenth and Nineteenth Centuries', *The Irish Ecclesiatical Record*, 5th series, vol. lxxii, September 1949, pp.255-264.

[128] Pollack, *op. cit.*, pp.332, 333.

CHAPTER FOUR
Ulster Protestants and the Restoration

[1] McIvor, *op.cit.* , p.34

[2] *op. cit.*, p.57

[3] Ó Casaide, *op. cit.*, p.48

[4] Sir Reginald Coupland, *Welsh and Scottish Nationalism*, London 1954, pp.188 ff.

[5] Ó Casaide, *op. cit.*, p.33

[6] Ó Buachalla, *I mBéal Feirsde Cois Cuain*, p.13

[7] S.N. MacGiolla Easpaig, *Tomás Ruiséil*, Dublin, 1957, pp.90, 213.

[8] M Scott, 'Ballymascanlon and Irish links with Gaelic Scotland', *Cuisle na nGael*, No.7, Newry, 1991, p.133

[9] Earnán de Blaghd, *op. cit.*, p.100

[10] Ó Buachalla, *op. cit.*, p.14

[11] Mac Con Midhe, *op. cit.*, Ó Casaide, *op. cit.*, p.91. Séamus Ó Néill, *op. cit.*, p.64, says Bryson did not attend the festival itself.

[12] Ó Buachalla, *op. cit.*, pp.18-25. Ó Néill, *op. cit*, p.61.

[13] Data culled from David Kennedy, 'James Mac Donnell 1762-1845', *Capuchin Annual*, 1945/6, pp.353-360.

[14] *Northern Star*, 16th-20th April 1795.

[15] Ó Buachalla, *op. cit.*, p.31. Mac Giolla Easpaig, *op. cit.*, p.91.

[16] R.A. Breatnach, *op. cit.*, p.145.

[17] Mary Mac Neill, *The Life and Times of Mary Ann McCracken*, Dublin, 1960, p.84.

[18] Proinsias Ó Conluain, *Dóchas Adtuaidh The North Began ...*, Dublin, 1944, p.4.

[19] *op. cit.*, p.8 (a reference to Tone writing out 30 Irish airs for the band of his regiment in France). Ó Néill, *op. cit.*, p.61.

[20] Ó Conluain, *op. cit.*, p.7. Seán Ua Cearnaigh, 'Jemmy Hope Stood for Civil Rights', *The Kerryman*, 26th May 1973. Ó Glaisne, *op. cit.*, p.4. P. Ó Snodaigh, 'Jemmy Hope', *Pobal*, October 1970. *Wolfe Tone Annual*, 1948, pp.84, 85. Among the books once owned by Jemmy Hope which have survived are a few in the National Museum of Ireland including his family Bible, Teeling's *Sequel ...* (a presentation copy) and Charles Vallancey's *An Essay on the Antiquity of the Irish Language ...* (London, 1818). For McCabe see R.R. Madden, *The United Irishman*, 3rd series, Vol. 1, Dublin, 1846, p.254. Ó Néill, *op. cit.*,

loc. cit., says that at the battle of Antrim when Hervey struck up the *Marseillaise*, Hope began a lively Irish air "which was soon taken up by the whole army".

21 M. Scott, 'Ballymascanlon and Irish Links with Gaelic Scotland', *Cuisle na nGael*, no. 7, 1991, p.133.

22 Ó Casaide, *op. cit.*, pp.18, 19. Ó Buachalla, *op. cit.*, pp.37, 38. Jackson, *op. cit.*, p.15.

23 7,697 in Belfast County Borough in 1911. Adams, *op. cit.*, p.117. Many of these must have been native speakers.

24 *Ordnance Survey Letters, Cavan/Leitrim*, p.103.

25 *Fermanagh*, p.26.

26 T.J. Barron to me, 27th July and 1st August 1972. One of Patrick Pearse's very few court cases, at the beginning of this century, involved his unsuccessful defence of a native Irish-speaker and member of the Gaelic League in the Donegal Gaeltacht who was charged with not having his name on his cart; he had, but being in Irish it was deemed non-existent in the eyes of the Law. (Liam Ó Connacháin, ed., *Niall Mac Giolla Bhríde*, 2nd edn., Dublin 1974, pp.76-85.)

CHAPTER FIVE
Restoration Belfast

1 *Transactions of the Gaelic Society of Dublin*. Vol. 1, 1808, p.1.

2 O'Flanagan, ed., *Advice to a Prince ... Being the Inauguration Ode of Donach Ó Broin*, Dublin, 1808, p.30.

3 Eoghan Ó Néill, *op. cit.*, pp.133, 189.

4 Ó Casaide, *op. cit.*, p.47.

5 David Kennedy, *op. cit.*, pp.357, 359.

6 J.H. Robb and J.R. Fisher, *Royal Belfast Academical Institution. Centenary Volume 1810-1910*, Belfast, 1913, p.209.

7 Ó Buachalla, *I mBéal Feirste Cois Cuain*, pp.43, 46-49.

8 p.49.

9 p.53.

10 pp.53-55

11 pp.59, 60.

[12] de Blácam, *op. cit.*, p.444.

[13] H.O. Mackey, ed., *Roger Casement, The Crime Against Europe*, Dublin, 1966, p.92. Casement was inveighing against gutter press attitudes echoing the tone set more archly by the *Times* in its hostility to what it described as "the artificial cultivation of Irish as the national language" (4th October 1882).

[14] Ó Buachalla, *op. cit.*, pp.65-68.

[15] pp.69-73. For a short account of MacAdam cf. Ruairí Ó Bléine, 'Roibeard Shipboy Mac Adaim', in B. Mhic Sheáin, eag., *Irisleabhar Uí Fhiaich*, 1993, pp.5-11.

[16] Anderson, *Historical Sketches of the Ancient Native Irish and their Descendents; Illustrative of their past and present state with regard to literature, education, and oral instruction,* 2nd edn., Edinburgh, 1830, p.210.

[17] Anderson, *op. cit.*, pp.270 ff. Cf. also Ó Baoill, *op. cit.*, p.166

[18] Ó Casaide, *op. cit.*, p.48.

[19] Ó Buachalla, *op. cit.*, p.p.73-77. (For Irish among other aristocrats, Clare and Castlereagh, see *Wolfe Tone Annual*, 1948, p.85).

[20] Ó Buachalla, *op. cit.*, pp.81-84. Ó Casaide, o*p. cit.*, pp.48, 49. T. Ó hAilín, 'Irish Revival Movement', in B. Ó Cuív, ed., *A View of the Irish Language*, pp.92, 93.

[21] Ó Buachalla, *op. cit.*, pp.86-88. Ó Casaide, *op. cit.*, p.50. Ó Néill, *op. cit.*, pp.43, 44.

[22] Ó Buachalla, *op. cit.*, pp.86-88. Ó Casaide, *op. cit.*, p.51.

[23] Ó Buachalla, *op. cit.*, pp.89-102.

[24] Ó Buachalla , *op. cit.*, p.91. Ó Casaide, *op. cit.*, pp.48, 49. Ó Muirí, *op. cit*, pp.64, 65.

[25] Ó Buachalla, *op. cit.*, pp.103-121.

[26] Ó Muirgheasa, *Dánta Diaga Uladh*, Dublin, 1969 edn., pp.350, 351. The same compilation has a long satire by Eoghan Ó Dubhthaigh about the confessionally mobile Bishop Myler McGrath and shows a correspondence between one line of it and a line of Patrick Dunkin's 'Truagh Mo Thuras Ó Mo Thír' which we have already mentioned—adding that it was likely Dunkin saw a copy of Ó Dubhthaigh's satire (p.308).

[27] Cf. Colm Beckett, *Aodh Mac Domhnaill—Poet and Philosopher*, Dundalk, 1987, p.18, and Réamonn Ó Muirí, *Lámhscríbhinní Staire an Bhionadaigh*, Éigse Oirialla, 1994.

[28] Seosamh Ó Duibhginn, *Séamus Mac Giolla Choille circa 1759-1829*, Dublin, 1972, p.8.

[29] Anna Heusaff, *op. cit.*, p.73. Séamas Mac Cuarta was another who wrote of the contention of the faiths in this area. Heusaff also marks the Protestant Hamilton family giving the site for a new Catholic chapel in Dundalk in 1750 (p.63). The English part of Mac Cumhaigh's macaronic poem was, it is said, written by John Short. For this and his marriage to Máire Ní Arbhasaigh see Damien Ó Muirí, *op. cit.*, p.182.

[30] Beckett, *op. cit.*, p.21, 22.

[31] Ó Buachalla, p.135.

[32] pp.136-157.

[33] Ó Buachalla, *op. cit.*, p.154.

[34] A. Mac Póilín, *op. cit.*, p.4.

[35] Muiris Ó Rocháin, 'Micheál Coimín, Gaelic Poet of Miltown Malbay (c. 1688-1760)', *Dál gCais*, no. 10, 1991, pp.59-69.

[36] A. Mac Póilín, *op. cit.*, *loc. cit.* Canon Cosslett Quin in Pilib Mistéil, ed., *op. cit.*, p.28. cf also Séamus Ó Cléirigh, *Feis na nGleann*, Ballycastle, 1995, p.6 where he draws on an article by Mac Neill never published in his lifetime but published posthumously in F.X. Martin and F.J. Byrne, *The Scholar Revolutionary*, Shannon, 1973, pp.323, 324.

CHAPTER SIX
Decline and Survival

[1] Ó Casaide, *op. cit.*, p.63.

[2] Ó Buachalla, *op. cit.*, *p.162.*

[3] Roger Blayney, 'Gaels of North Lead Revival', *Irish News* Centenary issue. The text reads:

Céad míle fáilte ar mhilliún don Bhanríon
Go Cúige Uladh na hÉire;
Go mba mharthanach slán a n-urraim is a dtáin di,
Le gean is le grá óna géillteáin

[4] Ó Néill, *op. cit.*, pp.63, 66.

[5] Éamonn de hÓir, *Seán Ó Donnabháin agus Eoghan Ó Comhraí*, Dublin, 1962, p.83.

[6] Ó Buachalla, *op. cit.*, p.p.272, 273. For a description of Ferguson see this summary of him by Gréagóir Ó Dúghaill in *Comhar*, April 1973,

p.19: "Ultach protastúnach, file, caomhach, Leas Choimeádaí na dTaifead Poiblí, Uachtarán Acadamh Ríoga na hÉireann, cúisitheoir don choróin i gCo. Ard Macha, etc., etc., fear a throid céad bliain ó shin le Coimisinéirí na Státseirbhíse ionas go mbeadh an Ghaeilge ina cháilíocht riachtanach ag iarrthóirí ar phoist ina oifig." Ó Dúghaill has published a full length study of him in *Samuel Ferguson, Beatha agus Saothar,* Dublin, 1993. See also his *Samuel Ferguson: An Introduction to his Life and Work,* FET, Belfast, n.d. (?1994)

[7] One major work compiled by Hugh Mac Donnell has been published: Colm Beckett, ed., *Fealsúnacht Aodha Mhic Dhomhnaill,* Dublin 1967.

[8] Ó Buachalla, *op. cit.,* p.272. Art Mac Bionaid's book on Irish history which led him to a breach with MacAdam has been published recently (1994) by Éigse Oirialla edited by Réamonn Ó Muirí.

[9] *The Nation,* 19th February 1848. (On the language in general see *The Nation,* vol. 2, p.72, 29th January 1848, where it is recorded that William Smith O'Brien was in favour. J.C. Mangan translated a poem of Ó Doirnín's in the same issue. On 26th February 1848 the *Scottish Gaelic Journal* is reported in *The Nation*).

[10] William Dillon, *Life of John Mitchel,* Vol. 1, London, 1888, p.8.

[11] Dillon, *op. cit.,* pp.2, 3. T.F. O'Sullivan, *The Young Irelanders,* Tralee, 1944, pp.477-479. Niall Ó Domhnaill, *Beatha Sheáin Mistéil,* Dublin, 1937, pp.7, 8.

[12] *The Nation,* 2nd March 1850.

[13] Réamonn Ó Muirí, *op. cit.,* pp.63, 64.

[14] Ruairí Ó Bléine, 'Roibeard Shipboy Mac Adaim (1808-1895), *Irisleabhar Uí Fhiaich,* 1993, p.9.

[15] Ó Buachalla, *op. cit.,* pp.222-231.

[16] Ó Néill, *op. cit.,* p.63. Frainc Ó Muirgheasa, 'Enrí Ó Muirgheasa— Cúlra an Fhir',in Ó Casaide, ed., *Énrí Ó Muirgheasa (1874-1945),* p.11.

[17] Ó Buachalla, *op. cit.,* p.162.

[18] *ibid,* p.272.

[19] McIvor, *Extracts from a Ballybay Schoolbook,* pp.43-45.

[20] Crone, *op. cit.,* p.141. His father also was an Irish-speaker. Cf. Seán Ó Luing, *Ó Donnabháin Rosa,* Vol. 1, Dublin, 1969, pp.187, 188.

[21] Tomás Ó Fiaich, 'Stair Nach Eol do Ultaigh', *Inniu,* 26th January 1973.

[22] For a short account see that by Séamas Ó Saothraí in *An tUltach,* February, 1973. A sustained tribute can be read in Mary Catherine,

Lady Ferguson's *Life of the Right Reverend William Reeves, DD, Lord Bishop of Down, Connor and Dromore*, Dublin, 1893.

[23] Ó Buachalla, *op. cit.*, pp.214, 215.

[24] Ó Buachalla, *op. cit.*, 216, 217. (Another reason of course for the undependablity in toto of the 1851 census is that, large numbers being illiterate, the constabulary filled out the forms on their behalf, Ó Dúghaill, *loc. cit.*).

[25] Ó Cuív, *Irish Dialects and Irish-speaking Districts*, Dublin, 1971, pp.22, 23.

[26] Ó Cuív, *op. cit.*, p.23-25.

[27] G.B. Adams, 'The Irish Language Census in Northern Ireland', in *Ulster Dialects*, p.111.

[28] P.L. Henry, *op. cit.*, p.147.

[29] Heslinga, *op. cit.*, p.107.

[30] Ó Cuív, *op. cit.*, p.23.

[31] Ó Néill, *op. cit.*, p.66, incorrectly assumed that MacAdam lived to see the first branch established. His brother, James, who shared his interest in things Irish predeceased him, dying in 1861.

CHAPTER SEVEN
Ulster Protestants and the Gaelic League

[1] *As I Roved Out*, Dublin, 1946, p.201.

[2] P. Ó Cléirigh, 'Rev. Euseby Digby Cleaver, M.A., (1826-1894)', *Rosc*, February 1973.

[3] G. Ó Dúghaill, 'Luathstair an Chonartha i mBéal Feirste', *An tUltach, November, 1971*.

[4] Mackey, *op. cit.*, pp.96,98.

[5] *Irish News* centenary issue (article by Roger Blayney).

[6] Ó Dúghaill, *op. cit., An tUltach,* January 1972.

[7] *ibid.*

[8] *ibid.*

[9] Lady Ferguson, *op. cit.*, p.28.

[10] Ó Glaisne, *op. cit.*, p.4.

[11] Horace Plunkett, *Ireland in the New Century*, London, p.157. Ó Glaisne, 'This is no Political Matter', *Studies*, Winter, 1993, p.8.

[12] *Irish Peasant*, 18th August 1906.

[13] *Inis Fáil*, January 1907.

[14] *Irish Nation and Peasant*, 17th July 1909.

[15] Ó Bléine, *loc. cit.*

[16] Rose, *op. cit.*, p.10.

[17] Adams, 'The Last Language Census in Northern Ireland', *oc. cit.*, p.139.

[18] *Rosc*, April 1971, p.3.

[19] R. Ó Glaisne, *Focus*, April 1966, pp.82, 83.

[20] Ó Glaisne, 'In Retrospect', *Search*, Vol. 12, no. 1, Spring 1989, pp.23-25, 27, 28.

[21] Giltrap, *op. cit.*, pp.37, 38, 55, 84.

[22] Charles Dickson to me, 6th September 1973. Uilliam Mac Artúir wrote a prefatory message for the Jubilee issue of *Fearsaid* (their journal), Belfast, 1956, p.7, where Seán Mac Airt gives a detailed history of the society, pp.9-19.

[23] *Q.C.B.*, 22nd February 1906.

[24] Conversation and notes of same, with Dr. Dickson, 1973, 1975.

[25] Mac Airt, *op. cit.*, p.11.

[26] 'Protastúnaigh agus Conradh na Gaeilge', in Liam Prút, ed., *Dúchas*, Dublin, 1990, pp.241, 243, 244.

[27] *op. cit.*, p.258.

[28] *Gleann Airbh go Glas Naíon*, Dublin, 1969, pp.46, 47.

[29] Séamus Ó Cléirigh, 'The Feis in the Glens of Antrim', *Rosc*, February 1973, p.2. Liam Mac Reachtain, 'Mná Protastúnacha agus an Ghaeilge', *Irish Press*, 19th May 1973. One of the 1970s county lieutenants, Dobbs, was a relative of Margaret Dobbs, *Inniu*, 6th June 1975.

[30] PRONI ms. T. 3072/1/2/4/4A/4B/6

[31] PRONI ms. D.1006/3/2/4/6/7/8/9/12/16/24/25/40/43/46.

[32] Cited from *Home Life in Ireland*, by Séamas Mac Páirc in 'Protastúnaigh an Tuaiscirt—Gaeil nó Gaill?', *Feasta*, August 1975, p.p.3-7. Lynd was also uncle to Conor Cruise O'Brien's first wife. For Milligan see Brighid Mhic Shéain, *Glimpses of Erin: Alice Milligan—Poet, Protestant and Patriot*, FET, Belfast, n.d. (?1994).

[33] *Saol*, July 1994, p.1.

[34] Register of Branches, Conradh na Gaeilge HQ, Dublin.

[35] Figures given in *Inniu*, 21st March 1975.

CHAPTER EIGHT
Modern Attitudes to the Language

1 'The Teaching of Irish History in Schools', *The Irish Teacher*, Winter 1970, p.18.

2 'The policy of the Presbyterian Church to the Gaelic Language', *The Christian Irishman, June 1965, p.63.*

3 M. Ó Droighneáin, ed., 'Éireannaigh—cad eile?' *An tUltach*, June, July 1962.

4 Roger Blayney, 'Gaels of North Lead Revival', in the *Irish News* Centenary Issue. Tarlach Ó hUid, 'Seo agus Siúd',*Clár Oifigeamhail Ath-thógáil Pháirc Uí Chorragáin*, Belfast, n.d. (?1946), p.57.

5 *Loyalist News, Ulster Constitution*, 26th August 1972.

6 *An tUltach*, June 1962.

7 *Irish Times*, Editorial, 21st February 1973.

8 Cf. letters of Pádraig Ó Conghaile and Diarmaid Mac Dáibhéid, *Irish Independent* 26st January 1973.

9 *Irish Times*, 3rd December 1980.

10 *The Orange Standard*, February 1980.

11 Magee, *op. cit.*, p.20.

12 One can also find an anti-Republican 1798 poem in Gaelic by one of the Breadalbane Fencibles, 'Oran a' Champa sa' Bhliadhna, 1798' (*Orain agus Dana Gaidhealach le Donnchadh Ban Mac an t-Saoir*, Edinburgh, 1859, pp.168, 169). For a larger discussion of 'Lilliburlero'— and much else of pertinence besides, cf. Ó Buachalla, 'Cing Séamas', *P.R.I.A.*, Vol. 83, C. 4, 1983.

13 *Pilib Mistéil, op. cit.*, p.7.

14 History, of course, records, contextualises, seeks to make the past understandable in its own terms to the present and for the future: it neither hides nor avoids the facts—at least it shouldn't! The underlay of British Israelism and the secularised and abbreviated version of it in some of Ian Adamson's work has been addressed by Anthony Buckley, 'We're Trying to Find our Identity: Uses of History among Ulster Protestants', in Tonkin, McDonald and Chapman, eds., *History and Ethnicity*, 1989—a study worthy of closer reading.

15 *Belfast Newsletter*, 29th June 1970.

16 *Éire-Ireland*, no. 833, Dublin, 15th September 1970. *Combat*, Vol. 1, no. 6, 25th April 1974, a UVF organ, in a note on an earlier edition of

the present work echoed many of its concluding sentiments thus:

> The majority of Ulster Protestants equate Gaelic and Irish culture with Roman Catholicism and are of the opinion that no 'good Prod' would have anything to do with such Popish traditions. The truth of the matter is, Ulster Protestants have as much claim, if not more in some cases, to the Gaelic culture as the Roman Catholic population. Someone once said that the Irish language was stolen from the Protestant people by the Papists; it would be more correct to say that the Protestant people gave their culture away to the Roman Catholics ... Gaelic culture is clearly the most important strand of Ulster culture; the music, poetry, songs, dances, stories and folklore—an inherited culture of 2,000 years—are all connected and still influence the lives of Ulster people.

17 'Orangemen Seek Sound of Gaelic' *Belfast Telegraph*, 28th June 1970

18 *To Irish Protestants*, Ara, Dublin, 1991, p.108.

19 In James McLoone, ed., *Being Protestant in Ireland*, Co-operation North, 1985, p.59.

20 *Memory and Redemption: Church Politics and Prophetic Theology in Ireland*, Dublin, 1993, pp.116, 117.

21 A. Pollak, *op. cit.*, p.334.

22 *Iontaobhas ULTACH: An Dara Tuairisc 1991-1993*, pp.5, 6.

APPENDIX
A Note on Education

1 McIvor, *Popular Education ...*, pp.21-34.

2 McIvor, pp.16-18

3 *ibid.*

4 cf. pp.17,61 *supra*

5 Donald F. MacDonald in the *Clan Donald Magazine*, No.3, 1965, p.19, says "Gaelic was proscribed as the language of the rebels and denounced as the 'Papist tongue'", and quotes Donald Mac Kinnon

(sometime ed. of the *Clan Mac Leod Magazine*) to the effect that "From the time of Queen Margaret and especially from 1603 when James VI became King of England there was a powerful influence exerted to make Scotland conform to English ways and usages in everything. The Stuart Kings were anti-Gaelic. It was James IV who smashed the Lordship of the Isles, the last bulwark of Gaelic culture in Scotland; and the writing of Gaelic names was made to conform to English ways". Under some of this pressure not only did Gaelic-speaking Scots move to Ireland but also to Carolina where the language has long since died out (Mac Donald, *op. cit.*, p.18) and to Cape Breton in Canada where it is still spoken in some areas (*Carn*, No. 10. August, 1975, pp.17, 18) as witness, say, the writings of Alasdair Mac Leod.

[6] John Lorne Campbell, *Gaelic in Scottish Education and Life*, Edinburgh, 1945, p.44.

[7] *ibid.*

[8] Scottish Council for Research in Education, Committee on Bilingualism, *Gaelic Speaking Children in Highland Schools*, London, 1961, p.17.

[9] Kearns, *op. cit*, p.24.

[10] T.C. Barnard, *op. cit*, p.259 fn. 49.

[11] There is no reference to any such provision in any of the appropriate authorities e.g. J. Coutts, *A History of the University of Glasgow*, Glasgow, 1909, where not only is there no reference in the index to Irish/Gaelic or Scots/Lallans but, we are informed that "Latin was the ordinary language used to communicate instruction" (p.173) and where it is also suggested that English may have been used as an auxiliary medium when in difficulties.

[12] William Boyd, *Education in Ayrshire Through Seven Centuries*, London, 1961, *passim.*

[13] Boyd, *op. cit.*, p.3.

[14] Campbell, *loc. cit.*

[15] John Kemp, D.D., *Extracts from an account of the Funds, Expenditure and General Management of the Affairs of the Society in Scotland for Propagating Christian Knowledge* ... Dublin, 1803, p.4.

[16] Ian J. Simpson, *Education in Aberdeenshire Before 1872*, London, 1947, p.156.

[17] *ibid.*

[18] *op. cit.*, p.157.

[19] Campbell, *op. cit.*, p.55.

[20] *op. cit.*, p.40.

[21] *op. cit.*, p.55.

[22] Kemp, *op. cit.*, p.25. Simpson, *op. cit.*, p.157.

[23] Simpson *loc. cit.*

[24] Simpson, *op. cit.*, p.158.

[25] *op. cit.*, p.162.

[26] Campbell, *op. cit.*, p.41.

[27] *Gaelic Speaking Children in Highland Schools*, p.17. cf. also Withers, *op. cit.*, pp. 5-7.

[28] R.L. Thompson, *The Study of Manx Gaelic*—the 1969 Rhys memorial lecture, offprinted from Vol. LV of the *Proceedings of the British Academy*, London, pp.184, 185, 207-209.

[29] Simpson, *op. cit.*, p.158.

[30] Tomás Ó Fiaich, *Má Nuad*, Maynooth, 1972, pp.62-64.

[31] Norman Mac Leod Jnr., in A. Clerk, LL.D., ed., *Caraid nan Gaidheal. The Friends of the Gael. A Choice Selection of Gaelic Writing by Norman Mac Leod, D.D.*, Edinburgh, 1910, pp.x, xxvi, xxxiii. Colm Ó Baoill, *op. cit.*, pp.159-168.

Index